LIBRARY LESSONS FOR Little Ones

UpstartBooks™

Janesville, Wisconsin

To Virginia Harrison, who made this book dream a reality;
my sister, Anne Sneed, a pioneer for quality care and instruction in Early Childhood Education;
my beloved grandsons, Ben and Alex, who will benefit from this book;
Teresa Sullivan, principal extraordinaire;
and to all the PPCD, pre-kindergarten, and kindergarten teachers of Tomball Independent School
District with whom I've worked to share the joy of literacy with little ones in the library lessons.

Published by UpstartBooks
401 S. Wright Road
Janesville, WI 53547
1-800-448-4887

© Aileen Kirkham, 2009
Cover design: Debra Neu

Table of Contents

Introduction

I hope this book will ignite and inspire the endless learning potential of children and those who educate them.

Motivation

My motivation for writing this book was to share an ongoing passion for quality instruction through the library and/or instructional classroom. With seven years experience in grades one, two, and five, and 20 years experience as a librarian, I've identified a critical need for library and classroom lessons that can:

- ignite the joy of reading in PK–K

- support the entire curriculum

- lend themselves to a co-teaching environment between the classroom and library

- be easily implemented by a librarian and/or teacher who has no prior experience with these age groups

- add to the expertise of seasoned veteran librarians

How To Use This Book

Lessons and Enrichment Activities

Versatile, dynamic lessons are the foundation of quality literature-based instruction. Given the limited attention spans of four- and five-year-olds, it is exceptionally important to provide lessons that are developmentally appropriate through the use of a "literacy variety show format" that incorporates activities, books, puppetry, songs, and Web site explorations. Curriculum connections are embedded throughout each lesson and provide ease of implementation in the public or school library and the instructional classroom. Each unit has a Story Lesson and an Enrichment Activity to complement the instructional objectives. This format offers the flexibility to addresses the various learning styles of your students.

Each Lesson Includes:

McRel Standards

The McRel Standards were developed by Mid-Continent Research for Education and Learning in Aurora, Colorado. McRel was incorporated in 1966 to "help educators ... bridge the gap between research and practice." The full list of standards can be found at www.mcrel.org/standards-benchmarks. The lessons in this book are primarily based on science and social studies objectives as well as some math, but also incorporate the following language arts and music standards:

Language Arts

- Reading

    –Uses the general skills and strategies of the reading process

    –Uses reading skills and strategies to understand and interpret a variety of literary texts

    –Uses reading skills and strategies to understand and interpret a variety of informational texts

- Listening

    –Uses listening and speaking strategies for different purposes

- Viewing

    –Uses viewing skills and strategies to understand and interpret visual media

- Media

    –Understands the characteristics and components of media

Music

—Sings, alone and with others, a varied repertoire of music

Objectives The McRel standards are broad national guidelines. Objectives are more measurable and more directly tied to the curriculum.

The Story Lesson

The lesson can be completed in 20 to 30 minutes.

Enrichment Activity

These vary from 20 to 30 minutes all the way through 60 minutes as a family program.

Resources

Resources were chosen to address a cross-section of ethnicities and subject matter. There are materials to satisfy each gender's interests, too. Due to the restrictive nature of many library budgets, the bibliography incorporates old and new book titles. Make the time to pull books related to the lesson and have them on display for students to check out after the lesson.

When sharing a nonfiction read-aloud, you may wish to "picture read" using captions only, or blend captions with some text from the page. Some nonfiction text is arduous to listen to, so decide what works best to make it developmentally appropriate for your group's attention span.

The Web sites are current as of this printing, but should an error message appear, perform a quotation mark or keyword search on the Web site title example: "www.aileenkirkham.com" or aileen kirkham. (There is another educator in the midwest with the same name, but I'm the Texan and the only one with the Web site.)

Optional: Create bookmarks with a graphic and titles of recommended books and Web sites for further reading pleasure at home.

Puppetry

Working with Puppets

When doing the puppetry, remember to always look at the puppet when it is talking to give the illusion it is real. The focus is on the puppet's face, not yours.

Making Puppets

Stick puppets are easy and inexpensive to make.

- Photocopy the patterns provided in this book onto cardstock/tagboard.
- Color, cut out, and glue the figures to the top of a paint stick. For durability, laminate before gluing.

Puppetry Etiquette for Children

- Hold the stick puppet in your hand as soon as you get it.
- Treat the puppet like a very special friend.
- Keep your puppet pal right beside you.
- Know that your puppet pal will have to go back to its safe place immediately if you choose to mishandle your puppet. (Fight with neighbor's puppet, tear up puppet, put puppet in neighbor's face, etc.)

Alphabet Fiesta

McRel Standards

Language Arts & Music

(Both listed in the Introduction on page 6.)

Lesson Objectives

- Sing songs to reinforce recognition of alphabet letters.
- Practice learning the names of the letters.
- Understand the need for alphabet letters to create words to read.
- Choose a book that teaches the sequential order of the ABCs.

Introduce the Lesson: The Reading Song

Preparation

- Make a story treasure chest or order from www.orientaltrading.com. If you want to make the chest, use a medium-sized box or hinged chest. Paint and glue on fake jewels; the shinier the better. The chest needs to be big enough to hold a large picture book and any props such as a puppet that goes with the story lesson.
- Use the pattern on page 11 to make a Rico Reader stick puppet.
- Make a transparency from page 12 to post the song words for the children to see.
- Display a list of the ABCs for the children to see.

Presentation

- Display the story treasure chest and provide three clues about what is inside.

- Call on three students to guess, and thank them for be willing to guess (affirms risk-taking).
- Peek inside the treasure chest, and slide your hand inside to grab the puppet.
- Make Rico pop out to surprise the children, announce his name, and tell the children he needs their help to sing *The Reading Song* today.
- Have Rico explain that it will be sung as an *echo* song. (Echo singing is when instructor/puppet sings first, then kids echo the same line.)
- Echo sing the *The Reading Song* on page 12 to the tune of the traditional ABC song.

Sharing the Story Lesson

Preparation

- Select a book from the recommended bibliography.
- Select and display an assortment of ABC books for students to check out later.

Presentation

- Read and share the alphabet book. If text is too lengthy, then briefly "picture read" each page for the students.
- Use Rico to teach the students the traditional version of the ABC song.

Checking for Understanding

- Ask students why they need to learn the names of the alphabet letters.
- Display Rico and challenge students to name the letter that starts each of Rico Reader's first and last name. Give help as needed.

- Direct students to the alphabet book display, and encourage them to check out and "picture read" an ABC book.

Extension Activity: Alphabet Song Sit

Preparation

- Make letter cards from patterns on pages 13–19 or have individual cards available with one alphabet letter per card. (Would recommend that these be laminated to reuse year after year.)
- Find a space for students to sit down in a circle.

Presentation

- Tell students to stand up in the circle.
- Explain that they will each receive an alphabet letter card.
- Direct them to listen for the name of their alphabet letter as the traditional ABC song is sung.
- Instruct them to sit down when they hear their letter's name. (You should walk around the circle to touch their shoulder if they don't know their letter and need help to know when to sit down.)
- Pass out the cards in alphabetical order.
- Sing and sit.

Check for Understanding

- Do the sing & sit a second time.
- Do a visual assessment of students to see who understands their letter name and sits at the appropriate time.
- If students need assistance, go to them, pronounce the letter's name, tap their shoulder, and point to the floor to cue them to sit.

Recommended Bibliography

Fiction

ABC Drive! A Car Trip Alphabet by Naomi Howland. Clarion Books, 1994.

Albert's Alphabet by Leslie Tryon. Aladdin Paperbacks, 1994.

Alligator Arrived with Apples: A Potluck Alphabet Feast by Crescent Dragonwagon. Aladdin, 1992.

Alphabet Adventure by Audrey Wood. Blue Sky Press, 2001.

Alphabet Mystery by Audrey Wood. Blue Sky Press, 2003.

Alphabet Rescue by Audrey Wood. Blue Sky Press, 2006.

Alphabet Under Construction by Denise Fleming. Henry Holt & Company, 2002.

Cleo's Alphabet Book by Stella Blackstone. Barefoot Books, 2006.

Click Clack, Quackity-Quack: An Alphabetical Adventure by Doreen Cronin. Atheneum, 2005.

Curious George Learns the Alphabet by H. A. Rey. Houghton Mifflin, 1973.

Dog's ABC: A Silly Story about the Alphabet by Emma Dodd. Puffin, 2003.

The Racecar Alphabet by Brian Floca. Atheneum, 2003.

Nonfiction

3D ABC: a Sculptural Alphabet by Bob Raczka. Millbrook Press, 2007.

A to Z, Do You Ever Feel Like Me?: A Guessing Alphabet of Feelings, Words and Other Cool Stuff by Bonnie Hausman. Dutton Children's Books, 1999.

ABC: A Child's First Alphabet Book by Alison Jay. Dutton Children's Books, 2003.

Achoo! Bang! Crash! The Noisy Alphabet by Ross MacDonald. Roaring Brook Press, 2003.

The Accidental Zucchini: An Unexpected Alphabet by Max Grover. Harcourt Brace, 1997.

Animal Babies ABC: An Alphabet Book of Animal Offspring by Barbara Knox. Capstone Press, 2003.

Brian Wildsmith's Amazing Animal Alphabet Book. Star Bright Books, 2008.

The Construction Alphabet Book by Jerry Pallotta. Charlesbridge, 2006.

Eating the Alphabet: Fruits and Vegetables from A to Z by Lois Ehlert. Harcourt, 1996.

Farms ABC: An Alphabet Book by B. A. Hoena. Capstone Press, 2005.

Into the A, B, Sea: An Ocean Alphabet by Deborah Lee Rose. Scholastic, 2000.

My Big Alphabet Book by Funfax, DK Pub., 1999.

Pets ABC: An Alphabet Book by Michael Dahl. Capstone Press, 2005.

The Turn-Around, Upside-Down Alphabet Book by Lisa Campbell Ernst. Simon & Schuster, 2004.

Zoopa: An Animal Alphabet by Gianna Marino. Chronicle Books, 2005.

Professional Books

101 Alphabet Activities: Ages 3–6 by Lisa Schwimmer Marier. Totline, 2004.

26 Easy & Adorable Alphabet Recipes for Snacktime by Tracy Jarboe. Scholastic, 2002.

ABC, Follow Me! Phonics, Rhymes and Crafts by Linda Armstrong. Linworth, 2007.

Alphabet Art: With A–Z Animal Art & Fingerplays by Judy Press. Williamson Pub., 1998.

The Alphabet Book: An ABC Book of Art, Rhymes, Patterns, and Activities by Sharon Ralph. Incentive Publications, 1995.

Learn-the-Alphabet Puppet Pals by Mary Beth Spann. Scholastic, 2003.

Library Story Hour from A to Z: Ready-to-Use Alphabet Activities for Young Learners by Ellen K. Hasbrouck. Jossey-Bass, 1998.

Numbers! Colors! Alphabet: A Concept Guide to Children's Picture Books by Melanie Axel-Lute. Linworth Pub., 2003.

Shoe Box Learning Centers' Alphabet by Jacqueline Clarke. Scholastic, 2006.

Multimedia (At the time of printing, all items were available from www.libraryvideo.com.)

ABC, 123, Colors & Shapes (Action Song Collection). Twentieth Century Fox, 2003.

Alphabet Fiesta. Nutmeg Media, 2004. (English & Spanish alphabet letters)

Alphabet Zoo (DVD Series). Brightstar Learning, 1994.

Animal Alphabet (Animal Alphabet & Number DVD Series). Time Life Records, 2002.

I Stink! Weston Woods, 2004.

Web Sites

IvyJoy.com's Learning the Alphabet Game www.ivyjoy.com/abc/abc.shtml. Click on an alphabet block to reveal words, pictures, and more related to that letter.

Oriental Trading www.orientaltrading.com. Inexpensive treasure chests.

PBS Kids: Sesame Street—Letter of the Day Game pbskids.org/sesame/letter/lettergame.html. Players drag and drop cookies starting with the letter of the day for Cookie Monster to eat.

Rico Reader Stick Puppet Pattern

Copy the pattern onto cardstock/tagboard. Then color, cut out, and glue it to the top of a paint stick to create a stick puppet. For durability, laminate before gluing.

The Reading Song

by Aileen Kirkham, ©2009

A, B, C, D, E, F, G.

Letters help me learn to read

With the book we'll share today

Letter names we'll learn to say

A, B, C, D, E, F, G

Letters help us learn to read.

Alphabet Card Patterns

Photocopy, laminate, and cut out cards.

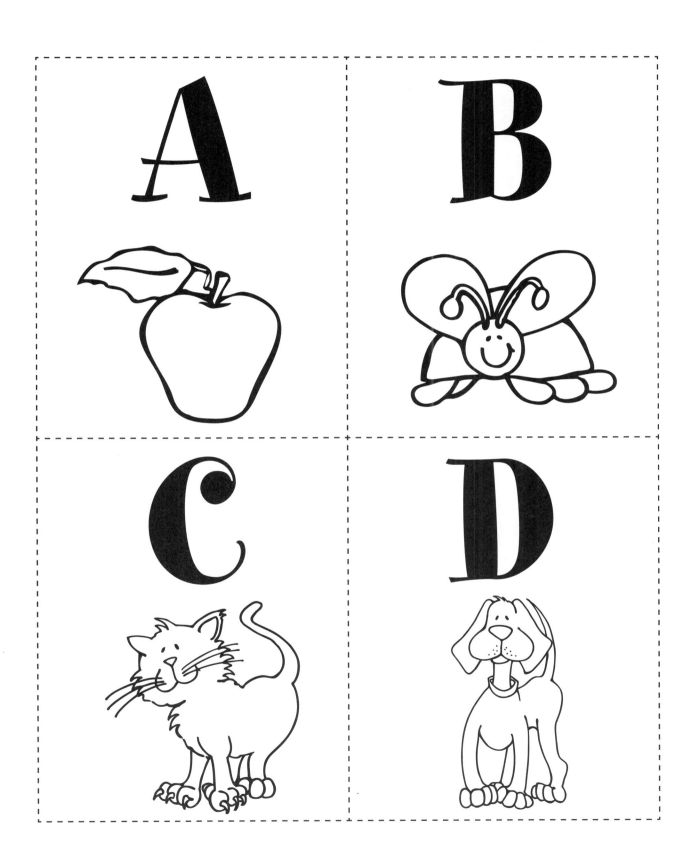

Alphabet Card Patterns

Alphabet Card Patterns

Alphabet Card Patterns

M

N

O

P

Alphabet Card Patterns

Alphabet Card Patterns

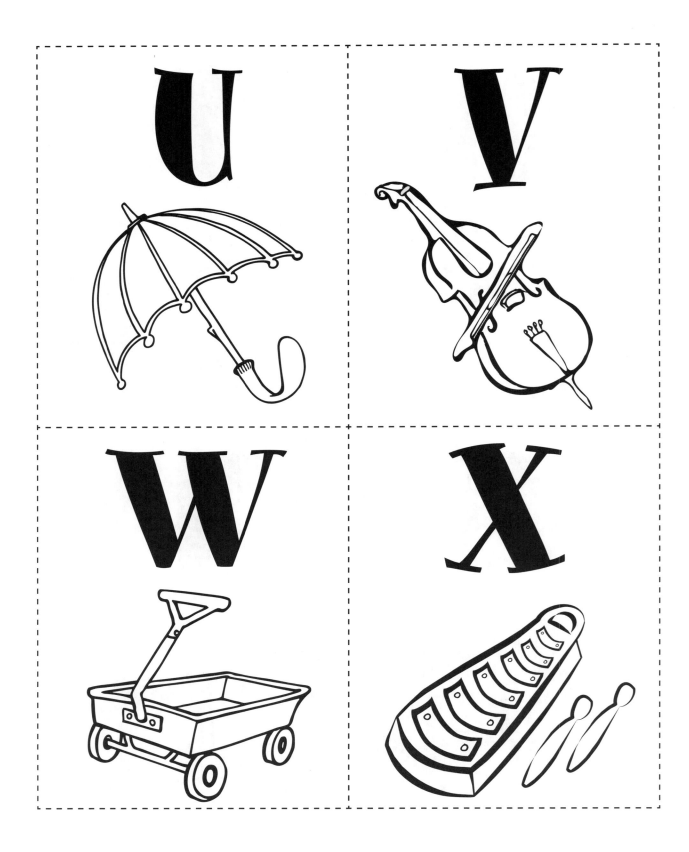

Alphabet Card Patterns

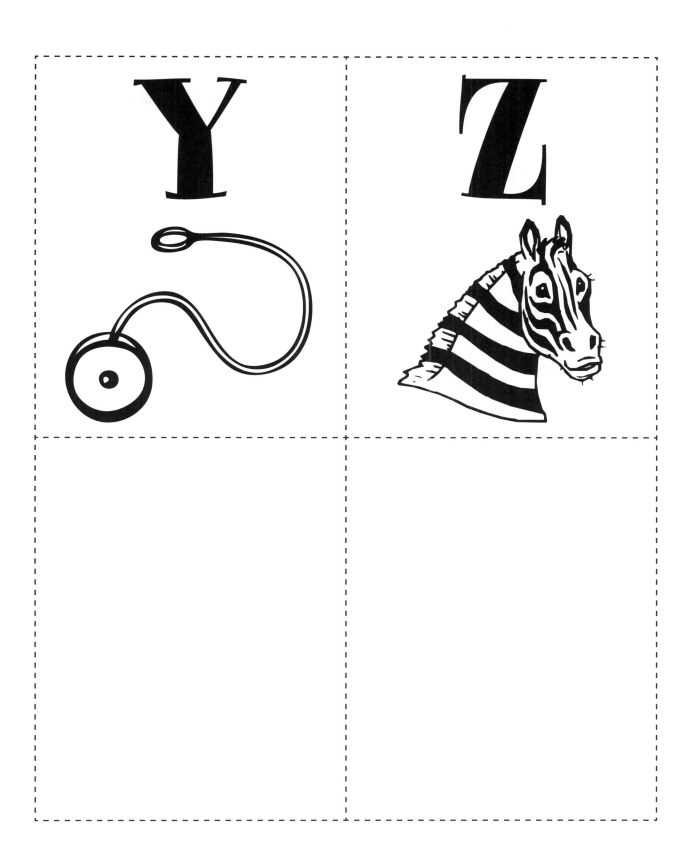

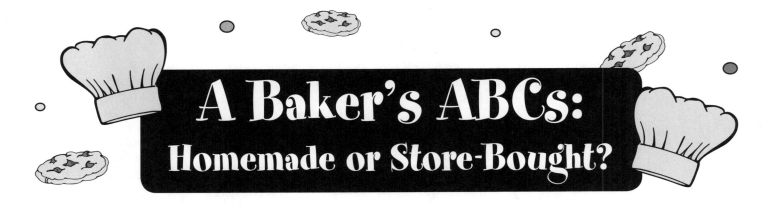

A Baker's ABCs:
Homemade or Store-Bought?

McRel Standards

Language Arts & Music

(Both listed in the Introduction on page 6.)

Grade K–4 History

- Understands family life now and in the past, and family life in various places long ago

Life Work

- Studies or pursues specific job interests
- Makes effective use of basic life skills

Mathematics

- Understands and applies basic and advanced properties of the concepts of measurements

Thinking and Reasoning

- Understands and applies the basic principles of logic and reasoning

Lesson Objectives

- Repeat the letter sound of **b**.
- Repeat the letter sound of **soft c**.
- Explore the steps necessary for baking.
- Identify the baker as a necessary community helper.
- Differentiate between the role of commercial bakers and homemade bakers.
- Follow sequential instructions.

Introduce the Lesson: Baking with the ABCs

Preparation

- Make the gingerbread cookie puppet using the pattern on page 23.
- Make a transparency of the *C Is for Cookies* song and the *C Is for Cookies* alphabet found on pages 24–25.

Presentation

- Tell the students they will sing a tasty letter song today. Direct them to say the letter sound when the six c's are sung together. Demonstrate by singing first, then having them echo each line.
- Use the gingerbread cookie puppet to help you sing the *C Is For Cookies* song on page 24.
- Explain that baking for family and friends requires lots of things to remember to do using the baker's ABCs.
- Review *C Is for Cookies* alphabet to explain the basics of cookie making.

Sharing the Story Lesson

Preparation

- Select and display a variety of baker- and cookie-themed books.

Presentation

- Read a cookie book aloud. Recommended title: *Mr. Cookie Baker*. Second choice options: *The Doorbell Rang* or *Who Ate All the Cookie Dough?*
- Share the fact that we bake some things at home, but most things are baked by a professional baker. Define homemade as baked

at home. Ready-made cookies, bread, and cakes that people buy were made by bakers.

Lesson Option

(Dependent upon attention span and time.)

- Picture read and discuss a nonfiction story about a commercial baker who bakes in massive quantities but still follows the ABCs of baking.

Check for Understanding

- Give scenarios and ask children if they would bake at home or buy them at the store. Tell them that some situations could have both answers*:

  1. Bread for all the schools to serve lunches each day. *(Store)*

  2. Cookies to put in your lunch kit. *(Store or Homemade)*

  3. Cookies for the daycare. *(Store or Homemade)*

  *Please note that more and more public venues such as daycares and schools require baked goods to be store bought due to concerns about transmission of hepatitis from homemade foods.

- Ask students to give reasons why bakers are an important part of our world.

- Encourage students to check out the baker and baked goods books.

Extension Activity: ABC Biscuits

Preparation

- Print out the ABC Biscuit recipe from kconnect.com/kc-ABCbiscuits.html.

- Request donations and/or purchase ingredients and cooking supplies.

- Borrow and/or bring from home the cooking equipment.

- Talk to the cafeteria manager about the availability of their ovens for this baking project.

- Contact parent helpers or older students to assist with activity. (If using student helpers, be sure to make enough for them, too.)

- Make a transparency of the *B is for Biscuit* song on page 26.

Sharing the Story Lesson

- Tell the students they will sing a tasty letter song today called *B Is for Buscui*ts on page 26. Direct them to say the letter sound when the six b's are sung together. Demonstrate by singing first, then having them echo each line.

- Give the instructions for making the ABC Biscuits.

- Assign each child/group a student/parent helper.

- Make the ABC Biscuits.

- Read *The Little Red Hen* aloud while the biscuits bake.

Checking for Understanding

- Ask the students to name the baker in the story.

- Ask the students to decide if the little red hen's bread was homemade or bought at the store.

- Ask the students if the biscuits made today were homemade or bought at the store. (Both answers are correct, since biscuit dough was bought at the store.)

- Enjoy the biscuits!

Recommended Bibliography

Fiction

Baker Cat by Posy Simmonds. Red Fox, 2006.

The Baker's Dozen: A Counting Book by Dan Andreasen. Holt, 2007.

Cinco Monitos Hacen un Pastel de Cumpleaños/Five Little Monkeys Bake a Birthday Cake by Eileen Christelow. Clarion Books, 2008. (Board Book)

The Doorbell Rang by Pat Hutchins. Mulberry, 1994.

Gingerbread Baby by Jan Brett. Putnam, 1999.

The Gingerbread Boy by Paul Galdone. Clarion Books, 1975.

The Gingerbread Cowboy by Janet Squires. Laura Geringer, 2006.

Gingerbread Friends by Jan Brett. Putnam, 2008.

The Gingerbread Girl by Lisa Campbell Ernst. Dutton Children's Books, 2006.

Harvey the Baker by Lars Klinting. Kingfisher, 2005.

If You Give a Mouse a Cookie by Laura Joffe Numeroff. HarperCollins, 2002.

The Little Red Hen by Byron Barton. HarperCollins, 1993.

The Little Red Hen by John Escott. Gingham Dog Press, 2003. (This version has hen using a commercial baker.)

Mr. Cookie Baker by Monica Wellington. Dutton, 2006.

This Little Bunny Can Bake by Janet Stein. Schwartz & Wade, 2009.

Walter the Baker by Eric Carle. Simon & Schuster, 2001.

Who Ate All the Cookie Dough? by Karen Beaumont. Henry Holt & Company, 2008.

Who Took the Cookies from the Cookie Jar by Bonnie Lass and Philemon Sturges. Little, Brown and Company, 2000.

Nonfiction

Baker by Dana Meachen Rau. Marshall Cavendish, 2008.

First Baking Activity Book by Helen Drew. DK Publishing, 2007.

Professional Books

The Doorbell Rang book guide for the book by Pat Hutchins. Scholastic, 2003.

Do You Know the Muffin Man? An Essential Preschool Literacy Resource by Pam Schiller and Thomas Moore. Gryphon House, 2004.

No Bake Cookies: More than 150 Fun, Easy, & Delicious Recipes for Cookies, Bars, and Other Cool Treats Made without Baking by Camilla V. Saulsbury. Cumberland House Publishing, 2006.

Web Sites

Classroom Cooking from Kindergarten Connection. kconnect.com/kc-ABCbiscuits.html. Easy biscuit recipe.

Cooking with Kids. www.childrensrecipes.com. Gingerbread baking recipes for use with children.

Gingerbread Cookie Puppet Pattern

Copy the pattern onto cardstock/tagboard. Then color, cut out, and glue it to the top of a paint stick to create a stick puppet. For durability, laminate before gluing.

C Is for Cookies

(Sung to the tune of *Where Is Thumbkin?*)

C is for cookies, C is for Cookies,
c, c, c, c, c, c,
Gather the ingredients.
Mix them all together.
Spoon them out.
Spoon them out.

C is for Cookies, C is for cookies,
c, c, c, c, c, c,
Cookies are delicious,
cookies are delicious,
Don't you agree?
Don't you agree?

C Is for Cookies Alphabet

A pron

B ake in heated oven

C ookie Sheets

D ough

E ggs

F lour

G et sugar

H ave butter

I ngredients

J ust measure carefully

K eep stirring in bowl

L eave spaces between dough on sheets

M ake teaspoon-size dough drops

N eed to set the timer

O ven check for browning

P otholders

Q uick to cook

R ecipe

S et out to cool

T aste for temperature

U s to eat them

V ery smart to eat only 1 or 2

W ash the Dishes

X tra fun to make and eat

Y ummy!

Z ip the bag to save the rest (zip-close bag)

B Is for Biscuits

(Sung to the tune of *Where Is Thumbkin?*)

B is for Biscuits, B is for Biscuits,

b, b, b, b, b, b,

Biscuits are delicious,

biscuits are delicious,

Eat some with me,

Eat some with me.

B Is for Biscuits

A pron

B ake in heated oven

C ookie Sheets

D ough

E xtra-large bowl

F lour

G et salt.

H ave butter

I ngredients

J ust measure carefully

K eep stirring in bowl

L eave spaces between dough on sheets

M ake biscuit-size dough drops

N eed to set the timer

O ven check for browning

P otholders

Q uick to cook

R ecipe

S et out to cool

T aste for temperature

U s to eat them

V ery good

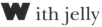

W ith jelly

X tra fun to make and eat

Y ummy!

Z ip the bag to save the rest (zip-close bag)

Birth and Earth Days

McRel Standards

Geography—Environment and Society

- Understands how human actions modify the physical environment

Grades K–4 History

- Understands the folklore and other cultural contributions from various regions of the United States and how they helped to form a national heritage

- Sings, alone and with others, a varied repertoire of music

Science—Life Sciences

- Understands relationships among organisms and their physical environment

Lesson Objectives

- Participate in a birthday book read-aloud to acknowledge a cultural tradition.

- Experience the potential of a variety of read-aloud opportunities.

- Discuss the rationale for having a recycling program.

- Implement a recycling program.

Introduce the Lesson

Preparation

- Buy or make an inedible birthday cake for display only.

Presentation

- Display and use the birthday cake as a prop to share information about your school's birthday book program as explained in the parent information letter on page 31.

- Sing *The Birthday Book Rhyme*, Verse 1:

The Birthday Book Rhyme

by Aileen Kirkham, ©2007

(Sung to the tune of *Ninety-nine Bottles of Beer on the Wall.*)

Verse 1

Happy, Happy Birthday,
I'll share this book with you,
Because of _____ (child's name) birthday, I hope you'll like it, too. Enjoy!

Sharing the Story Lesson

Preparation

- Find a space to display a box of new books. Children may choose a title for their birthday book read-aloud.

- Copy and cut out pattern for cupcake bookplates from page 32.

- Make a cupcake bookplate to honor your own birthday to use as a sample each year. Write your name and birth month and day on the cupcake. Glue or attach with contact paper onto the inside of your birthday book.

- Copy the Birthday Book Parent Letter to send home to parents found on page 31.

Presentation

- Identify the title of the book, author, and illustrator.

- Open the book, show the birthday cupcake bookplate, and read the name and date on the cupcake.

- Read the birthday book aloud. (Book does not have to be a birthday themed book, but the bibliography will reflect that since you'll need a sample book for demonstration for this lesson.)

- Discuss, as time permits, any curriculum connection that can be made.

Checking for Understanding

- Sing *The Birthday Book Rhyme*, Verse 2:

Verse 2

Thank you, thank you, thank you,
for your birthday book,
Now you can take it home with you
for your family to read and look. Enjoy!

(If students don't take home books, change wording to:

Now you can take it to your class

for all to read and look. Enjoy!)

- Show them the Birthday Book parent letter. Explain the program and direct them to take the letter home and give it to their parents. Be sure to emphasize the fact that the birthday book program is **optional**.

- Give class sets of letters to teachers to distribute at the end of the day.

Extension Activity: Recycling Project

Preparation

- As you throw your boxes and cans into the recycling bin, remember to save the box tops and soup labels!

- Set up and label containers for a recycling center in a centrally located area.

(I use tall kitchen trashcans with plastic liners, but covered boxes work just fine.)

Example

1. *Boxtops for Education.* www.boxtops4education.com

2. *Campbell's Labels.* www.labelsforeducation.com

3. *Cartridges for Kids Program.* www.cartridgesforkids.com

4. *Tyson's A+ Program.* www.tyson.com/projectaplus

5. Gently used books can recycle into your library collection, classroom collections, and/or book walk prizes for family night.

- Make a transparency of *The Recycling Song* from page 33.

Presentation

- Display the birthday cake and suggest that in some ways, the earth has a birthday every time the sun comes up because a new day is born.

- Ask kids to define the reason for giving a gift (care about someone, appreciation, concern, etc.).

- Display words and sing *The Recycling Song* on page 33.

- Discuss the meaning of the song's words as being a way to show the earth we care and celebrate its many birthdays.

- Take the children to the recycling center and show them samples of items that go in each container. Model with actions how to bring in the items and drop them in the containers.

- Encourage them to speak to family members, friends, and neighbors to help them collect donated items to bring to school.

- Share the fact that one bonus of recycling is refunded money, and/or items the school will earn–especially when the refunded money buys a "newborn" book for the library!

- Read a book aloud that you bought with recycling money.

Recommended Bibliography

Fiction

Big Brown Bear's Birthday Surprise by David McPhail. Harcourt, 2007.

A Birthday Basket for Tia by Pat Mora. Aladdin, 1997.

The Birthday Box: Happy Birthday to Me! by Leslie Patricelli. Candlewick Press, 2007.

The Birthday Car by Margaret Hillert. Norwood House Press, 2007.

The Birthday Fish by Dan Yaccarino. Henry Holt & Company, 2005.

Buzzy's Birthday by Harriet Ziefert. Blue Apple Books, 2004.

Clifford's Birthday Party by Norman Bridwell. Scholastic, 1988.

Earth Day Birthday by Pattie L. Schnetzler. Dawn Publications, 2004.

Every Year on Your Birthday by Rose A. Lewis. Little, Brown and Company, 2007.

The Giant Hug by Sandra Horning. Knopf, 2005.

Happy Birthday, Biscuit! by Alyssa Satin Capucilli. HarperCollins, 1999.

Happy Birthday Chimp and Zee by Laurence Anholt. Frances Lincoln, 2006.

Happy Birthday, Davy! by Brigitte Weninger. North-South Books, 2004.

Happy Birthday, Dear Duck by Eve Bunting. Clarion Books, 1988.

Happy Birthday, Jamela! by Niki Daly. Farrar, Straus and Giroux, 2006.

Happy Birthday, Little Red Riding Hood! by Alma Flor Ada. Alfaguara, 2002.

Happy Birthday, Moon by Frank Asch. Aladdin Paperbacks, 2005.

Happy Birthday to Me by David and Tessie DeVore. CharismaKids, 2004.

January's Child: The Birthday Month Book by Andrea Alban Gosline. Scholastic, 2007.

Jimmy's Boa and the Big Splash Birthday Bash by Trinka Hakes Noble. Dial, 1989.

Moira's Birthday by Robert Munsch. Annick Press, 1992.

Otto Has a Birthday Party by Todd Parr. Little, Brown and Company, 2004.

Pip & Squeak by Ian Schoenherr. Greenwillow Books, 2007.

Recycle Every Day! by Nancy Elizabeth Wallace. Marshall Cavendish, 2006.

The Secret Birthday Message by Eric Carle. HarperCollins, 1998.

Nonfiction

A 3-D Birthday Party by Ellen B. Senisi. Children's Press, 2007.

Let's Recycle! by Anne L. Mackenzie. Capstone Press, 2007.

Watch Me Make a Birthday Card by Jack Otten. Children's Press, 2002.

Why Should I Recycle? by Jen Green. Barron's, 2005.

Multimedia (At the time of printing, all items were available from www.libraryvideo.com.)

The Toy Castle: Birthday Bash. Questar, 2006.

Party Time with Max & Ruby. Paramount Pictures, 2006.

Play Time Maisy. Universal Studios, 2004.

Me, Eloise. Anchor Bay, 2006.

Web Sites

Boxtops for Education. www.boxtops4education.com. Everything you need to know about this fundraiser.

Campbell's Labels. www.labelsforeducation.com. Everything you need to know about this fundraiser.

Cartridges for Kids Program. www.cartridgesforkids.com. Everything you need to know about this recycling fundraiser.

Kids Domain—Birthday Fun. party.kaboose.com/party-favors. Easy crafts to make at birthday parties.

IvyJoy.com's Learning the Alphabet Game. www.ivyjoy.com/abc/abc.shtml. Click on an alphabet block to reveal words, pictures, and more related to that letter.

Tyson's A+ Program. www.tyson.com/projectaplus. Everything you need to know about this fundraiser.

Birthday Book Parent Letter

Child's Name _____   Teacher's Name _____

Child's Birthday _____

Birthday Book Program

Date _____

Dear families of _____,

The birthday book program offers your family the option of sending $_____
(average cost of a new hardback book) to honor you child's birthday. Should you wish
to do this, send cash or check payable to_____.
Place the money with this form in an envelope, and ask your child to deliver the
envelope to the library.

In return for this payment, your child will get to:

1. Pick a book from the birthday book basket.

2. Have a cupcake bookplate placed inside the book with his/her name on it.

3. Wait for the day of the birthday book appointment.

4. Have the story read aloud to his/her class.

5. Take the book home for the book's <u>first time to be checked out</u> and share it
    with his/her family.

6   Return the book to the library for all the other students to use in the future.

7. Be remembered for sharing and caring for other students with this book
    contribution to the library when kids see the birthday cupcake bookplate.

Thank you,

_____

Cupcake Bookplate Pattern

Copy on colored cardstock or use brightly colored paper.
Cut out and keep on file for use in future birthday books.

Rico Reader
January 1, 2009

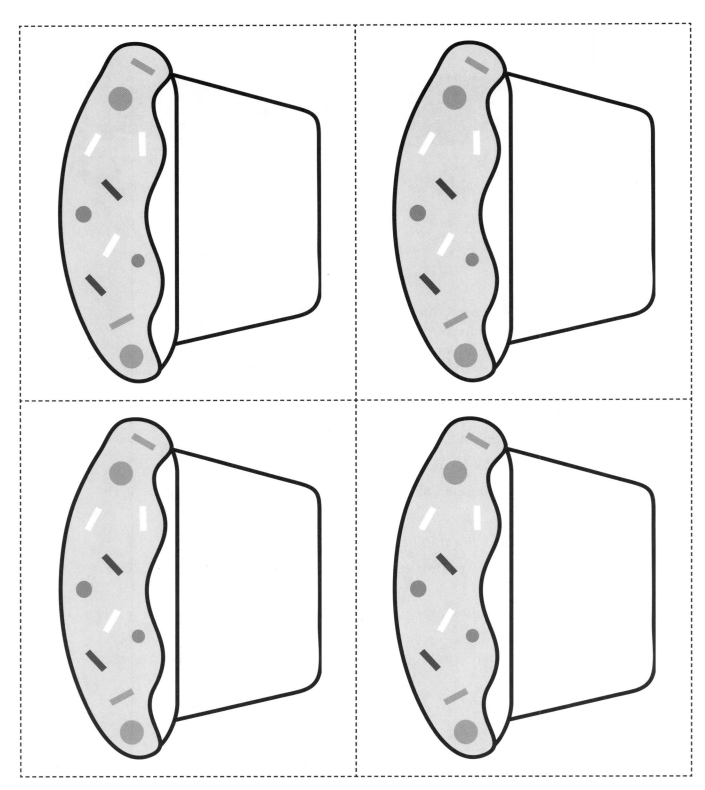

The Recycling Song

(Sung to the tune of *A Hunting We Will Go.*)

Recycle, recycle, recycle,

make trash turn into cash.

Recycle, recycle, recycle,

make the beauty of

our earth last.

Body Divine:
Wash Time

McRel Standards

Language Arts & Music

(Both listed in the Introduction on page 6.)

Health

- Knows how to maintain and promote personal health

Theater

- Uses acting skills

Lesson Objectives

- Name parts of the body.

- Sequence body parts from head to toe.

- Use spatial terminology to define body part locations.

- Define the purpose of body parts.

- Use letter sounds to reinforce the two necessities for bathing body parts: soap and water.

- Dramatize bathing the body parts.

- Identify the need for a daily bath.

Introduce the Lesson: Body Mine

Preparation

- Make a transparency of the song, *Body Parts that Meet* on page 37.

Presentation

- Display, sing, and dramatize *Body Parts that Meet.*

Sharing the Story Lesson

Preparation

- Select and display a variety of fiction and nonfiction books about body parts. *Parts* and *It's My Body's ABC* are needed for the lesson.

Presentation

- Read *Parts* aloud and discuss the fact that the body is alive and constantly changing. Ask the children to make observations about how their own bodies have changed in addition to teeth, hair, and skin. (Give clues: need new shoes, clothes, haircuts, etc.)

- Picture read a nonfiction book such as *It's My Body's ABC* to enhance the understanding of body parts and their purposes.

Check for Understanding

- Display, sing, and dramatize *Body Parts that Meet* again.

- Ask students to play the game, *What Part Am I?* Direct the students to touch the body part that matches the oral description that you give. Visually assess the students as they do the action song to see which students demonstrate the 1–1 correspondence of the body part with its name.

What Part Am I?

1. The part of your body that has your ears, eyes, nose, mouth, and holds your brain to think. *(Head)*

2. The part of your body that is between your head and your torso. (Define while pointing to torso.) *(Neck)*

3. The parts of your body that your arms are connected to. *(Shoulders)*

4. The parts of your arms that allow them to bend. *(Elbows)*

5. The parts of your legs that allow them to bend. *(Knees)*

6. The parts of your body that are attached to the bottom of your legs and are used for walking. *(Feet)*

Extension Activity: You Stink!

Preparation

- Bookmark the Web site, kids.niehs.nih. gov/lyrics/thumbkin.htm.

- Make the sponge puppet on page 38.

- Make the soap puppet on page 39.

- Make a transparency of the song, *You Stink!*, for kids to see and sing along—on page 40.

Presentation

- Display, sing, and dramatize the action song, *Where is Thumbkin* from: kids.niehs. nih.gov/lyrics/thumbkin.htm. Explain that Thumbkin and the other finger friends are the body parts that use two tools to keep your body from smelling stinky: water AND soap. Put a heavy emphasis on the soap since some kids think they can get clean using only water.

- Read a recommended bath book from the bibliography aloud. (If you choose *Ten Dirty Pigs* ..., note the fact that pigs actually need the mud to stay cool, kids don't!)

- Display the lyrics to the song *You Stink* on page 40 to introduce it, and then dramatize the song as if standing in the shower, using the sponge and soap puppets. (Explain that the sponge holds the water to wash with the soap.)

- Make note of what areas are easy to overlook, and can get very dirty.

  Sequence from top to bottom (feet):

  1. Head – behind and inside of ears

  2. Neck – creases under head

  3. Shoulders/Arms – underarms

  4. Elbows – inside

  5. Knees – behind

  6. Feet – between toes

- Sing the song, *You Stink!*, again and pantomime cleaning these areas.

Check for Understanding

What starts with the S sound (make S sound) and washes off smells? *(Soap)*

What starts with the W sound (make sound of W) that washes off the soap and the smells? *(Water)*

How often should you use these two things? *(Everyday)*

Who needs to take a bath? *(Everybody)*

Recommended Bibliography

Fiction

All Dirty! All Clean! by Harriet Ziefert. Sterling Publishing, 2005.

Bath Time by Eileen Spinelli. Marshall Cavendish, 2003.

Bernard's Bath by Joan E. Goodman. Boyds Mills Press, 2000.

Big Smelly Bear by Britta Teckentrup. Sterling Publishing, 2008.

Kid Tea by Elizabeth Ficocelli. Marshall Cavendish, 2008.

Parts by Tedd Arnold. Puffin, 2000.

Ten Dirty Pigs; Ten Clean Pigs: An Upside-Down, Turn-Around Bathtime Counting Book by Carol Roth. North-South Books, 2002.

Who's in the Tub? by Sylvie Jones. Blue Apple Books, 2007.

Nonfiction

Dirty and Clean by Melinda Lilly. Rourke Publishing, 2004.

Head, Shoulders, Knees, and Toes: And Other Action Rhymes by Zita Newcome. Candlewick Press, 2002.

It's My Body ABC by Lola M. Schaefer. Heinemann Library, 2003.

Keeping Your Body Clean by Mary Elizabeth Salzmann. Abdo Pub., 2004.

Taking My Bath by Elizabeth Vogel. Rosen Publishing Group, 2003.

Web Site

Niehs Kids' Pages: Sing Along Songs. kids.niehs.nih.gov/lyrics/thumbkin.htm. Lyrics and melody for *Where Is Thumbkin?*

Body Parts That Meet

(Sung to the tune of *99 Bottles of Beer on the Wall.*)

Head, neck, and shoulders,

(Sing the words and use both hands to touch the parts.)

Elbows, knees, and feet,

(Sing the words and use both hands to touch the parts.)

From head to toe,

(Use both hands and start at head, then sweep hands down to toes.)

I need to know

(Point to brain.)

My body parts that meet.

(Use both hands and start at head to sweep hands down to toes.)

Sponge Puppet Pattern

Copy the pattern onto cardstock/tagboard. Then, color, cut out, and glue it to the top of a paint stick to create a sponge on a stick washing "tool." For durability, laminate before gluing.
Option: Go to a dollar store and get a real sponge and glue facial expressions on it.

Soap Puppet Pattern

Copy the pattern onto cardstock/tagboard. Then, color, cut out, and glue it to a real soap box that's been covered with paper to match the color of the cardstock/tagboard cutout, or glue it to the top of a paint stick. For durability, laminate before gluing.

Option: Ask staff members to save complimentary soaps from hotel stays and give them to you for use in this lesson. If you get enough, give each child a soap to take home and use.)

You Stink!

(Sung to the tune of the refrain of Handel's *Messiah.*)

Soap and water,
soap and water,
yes, you oughta
use it each and everyday.

Soap and water,
soap and water,
yes, you oughta
use it
each and everyday.

Friends will appreciate that you
have no smell and
will never ever have to say
… YOU STINK!

Caldecott: Medals & Parts

McRel Standards

Language Arts & Music

(Both listed in the Introduction on page 6.)

Grades K–4 History

- Understands the folklore and other cultural contributions from various regions of the United States and how they helped form a national heritage

Lesson Objectives

- Recognize quality illustrations in literature.
- Differentiate between authors and illustrators.
- Discuss the criteria for winning a Caldecott medal. *Most distinguished American Pic book*
- Identify the location of the list of Caldecott books (poster).
- Learn the names of the basic parts of a book.

Introduce the Lesson: Caldecott Medals

Preparation

- Borrow or buy a gold and a silver medal. (Oriental Trading has very inexpensive ones.)
- Make a transparency from page 45 of the *Caldecott Song* for students to see and sing along.
- Color code the library's Caldecott medal books. (I use a ¾" yellow dot, write the year it was selected as a medalist, and tape it to the spine.
- Select and display age-appropriate Caldecott winner and honor books:

Winners: Gold Medalists for Read-Aloud

1. *Drummer Hoff*—unique woodcut illustrations. Tell kids each one of these pictures was made with many wooden stamps. Each color on the page required a new stamp to be cut out of wood and dipped in paint to stamp on the big picture. Can have kids do a repetitive refrain after each page. "Fire It Off!"

2. *Frog Went a Courtin'*—older title, but can be sung or read. It's a classic tale of predator vs. prey, with the prey ultimately escaping and living happily ever after.

3. *The Funny Little Woman*—Japanese story with famous Japanese monsters, Oni. The woman outsmarts them.

4. *The Hello, Goodbye Window*—special window at grandparents house lets a little girl see everyone coming and going.

5. *Joseph Had a Little Overcoat*—perfect story to teach reusing old clothes instead of always buying new.

6. *Kitten's First Full Moon*—kitten mistakes the moon for a bowl of milk.

7. *Officer Buckle and Gloria*—excellent for teaching safety rules.

Honor Books: Silver Medalists for Read-Aloud

1. *Alexander and the Wind-up Mouse*—a tale of friendship.

2. *Alphabatics*—each alphabet letter turns into an object.

3. *Color Zoo*—uses various shapes and vibrant colors to create zoo animals.

4. *Don't Let the Pigeon Drive the Bus*—goofy humor the kids love.

5. *Ella Sarah Gets Dressed*—a strong-willed child dresses herself even though it may not be the best look for her.

6. *Frederick*—a poetic mouse shares his poems to help his friends through the winter.

7. *Have You Seen My Duckling*—Mother Duck looks for her lost duckling.

8. *Hondo & Fabian*—two pets and their daily doings.

Presentation

- Hold up the medals and ask kids if they've ever won a prize like a medal, a trophy, a stuffed animal, etc.

- Discuss and share reasons for their prizes.

- ~~Explain the fact that the gold and silver Caldecott medals are very special book prizes.~~

- ~~Tell them to listen to the *Caldecott Song* on page 45 to find out why a book wins the Caldecott medal.~~

- Direct the children to echo sing the song. Tell them you will sing first, then they will repeat the line.

- Ask them to remember the song's words to remind them why a book to wins the Caldecott medal. (pictures)

- Share visual cues they can use to identify Caldecott books—color-coded label on spine and/or the location of Caldecott winners poster.

Sharing the Story Lesson

Preparation

- Maintain the Caldecott book display for the lesson and for kids to check out from after the lesson.

Presentation

- Select a Caldecott book to read aloud and share the pictures.

- Optional: Check your interlibrary loan service to order or purchase the DVD listed in this section's bibliography from www.libraryvideo.com so the pictures can "come alive" with animation. Select and show one book.

Check for Understanding

- Use the transparency to sing the *Caldecott Song* again to review why a book receives a Caldecott medals.

- Assess the students' learning by asking them to show thumb signals for responses:

  1. Thumbs up if the Caldecott medal is for the best pictures.

  2. Thumbs sideways if they're not sure.

  3. Thumbs down if the Caldecott medal is for the best words in the story.

- Discuss their answers to reinforce the concept of pictures as the winning criteria.

- Review with students how the Caldecott books are identified in the library: color coded stickers and/or the winners' poster.

- Encourage students to select Caldecott books to check out.

Extension Activity: What Part Is This?

Preparation

- Get the book, *Joseph Had a Little Overcoat.* Be sure it has a color-coded sticker on it to show it is a Caldecott medalist.

- Write seven blanks on the board to fill in each letter of the word, Library, during the "Check for Understanding" section.

  Optional: Check your interlibrary loan service to order or purchase the DVD listed in the bibliography. The DVD includes the song that matches the story.

Story Lesson

- Read the story or show it on DVD.

- Make the analogy that Joseph took something big and reused it to make it into a different thing that was helpful to him.

- Share the fact that books also have helpful parts. Show where the part can be found, and explain their purpose. Be sure to say the part aloud and have the kids repeat it.

  1. Front Cover – protects the pages at the front of the book.

  2. Back Cover – protects the pages at the back of the book.

  3. Spine – glue or sewing thread is used to keep the pages together and in order.

  Note: I like to have the kids touch their own spines and ask them what purpose it serves. Discuss the fact they'd be like jello on the floor if their body didn't have a spine to keep their bones in place. If a book didn't have a spine, the pages would fall out and they wouldn't keep their shape inside the covers.

  4. Spine Label – address of the book, so you know where it lives in the library.

  5. Caldecott Sticker – tells you the book has won the picture book prize.

  6. Pages – contain the words and the pictures.

  7. Title Page – tells you the name of the book, the author, and the illustrator.

Check for Understanding

- Tell the kids they are ready to play the *Book Parts Game*.

- Tell them that for every correct answer they give, you will fill in a missing part (letter) of an important word: _ _ _ _ _ _ _ (*Library*)

- Point to a part of the book and ask them what it is. If extra help is needed to remember this new information, give them the sound of the letter at the beginning of the answer word and other clues as necessary.

- Congratulate them on naming the parts of the book and filling in the parts of the missing word.

- Encourage them to use the important word, "Library," to find Caldecott medal books to check out.

Recommended Bibliography

Fiction

Alexander and the Wind-up Mouse by Leo Lionni. Scholastic, 1999.

Alphabatics by Suse MacDonald. Aladdin, 1992.

Don't Let the Pigeon Drive the Bus by Mo Willems. Hyperion Books for Children, 2003.

Ella Sarah Gets Dressed by Margaret Chodos-Irvine. Harcourt, 2003.

Frederick by Leo Lionni. Random House, 1973.

Have You Seen My Duckling? by Nancy Tafuri. Greenwillow Books, 1984.

Hondo & Fabian by Peter McCarty. Henry Holt & Company, 2002.

The Hello, Goodbye Window by Norton Juster. Hyperion, 2005.

Joseph Had a Little Overcoat by Simms Taback. Viking, 1999.

Kitten's First Full Moon by Kevin Henkes. Greenwillow Books, 2004.

Officer Buckle and Gloria by Peggy Rathmann. Scholastic, 1996.

Nonfiction

Color Zoo by Lois Ehlert. Trumpet Club, 1990.

Drummer Hoff by Barbara Emberley. Aladdin, 2005.

Frog Went a-Courtin' by John Langstaff. Scholastic, 1989.

The Funny Little Woman by Arlene Mosel. Penguin Group, 1993.

Randolph Caldecott's Picture Books by Randolph Caldecott. Huntington Library, 2008.

Professional Books

Newbery and Caldecott Medal and Honor Books in Other Media by Paulette Bochnig Sharkey. Neal-Schuman Publishers, 1992.

Multimedia

Strega Nona … and More Caldecott Award Winning Folk Tales from Scholastic, 2001. DVD or VHS.

Web Sites

Library Video. www.libraryvideo.com. National distributor of educational videos, DVDs, and audiobooks to schools and public libraries.

Oriental Trading. www.orientaltrading.com. Inexpensive gold and silver medals.

Caldecott Song

(Sung the tune of *Row, Row, Row Your Boat.*)

Cal, Cal, Caldecott

medal on a book,

Means it's won the picture prize

so take another look.

Fact or Fiction: Frog or Toad?

McRel Standards

Language Arts & Music

(Both listed in the Introduction on page 6.)

Science—Life Science

- Understands the relationships among organisms and their physical environment
- Understands biological evolution and the diversity of life

Lesson Objectives

- Distinguish the difference between fact and fiction books.
- View and hear the physical attributes of frogs and toads.
- Dramatize the movement of frogs.
- Participate in frog movements to demonstrate spatial terminology.

Introduce the Lesson

Preparation

- Make the frog and toad construction paper puppets using the pattern directions on pages 49–50.
- Make a transparency from page 51 of the *Books Are Great!* song for students to see and sing along.
- Bookmark the Web site, www.naturesound.com/frogs/frogs.html.
- Read the San Diego Zoo article on Amphibians: *Frog & Toad* at www.sandiegozoo.org/animalbytes/t-frog_toad.html.

Presentation

- Show the *Frogs and Toads in Color and Sound* Web site and click on a few of the frogs and toads one at a time to hear their individual sounds.
- Display the transparency of the *Books Are Great!* song.
- Ask kids to compare the Web site and the transparency and decide if the Web site or the transparency shows frogs in real life.
- Use the frog and toad paper puppets to sing this introductory song *Books Are Great!* on page 51.

Sharing the Story Lesson

Preparation

- Select and display a variety of fiction and nonfiction frog and toad books.
- Label two boxes with large letters:
  1. Pretend = Fiction
  2. True = Nonfiction

Presentation

- Explain that book covers often let you know if the books are true or pretend. Point to the boxes to show the library words for these terms:

  Pretend = Fiction, True = Nonfiction.

- Share frog and toad attributes: frogs tend to have longer legs, tend to live near water, and have moist, smooth skin. Toads tend to have drier, bumpy skin, shorter legs, and are usually heavier than a frog (except a bullfrog).

- Hold up two library books: one that is fiction about frogs and/or toads and one that is nonfiction about frogs and/or toads. Ask students to point to the book they believe will have more true information about frogs and/or toads, and the book that has more imaginary information about them. (Helpful hint: most nonfiction books use true-to-life photos; kids can relate to photos.)

Place the fiction book in the Pretend = Fiction box.

- Discuss and read aloud or picture read the nonfiction book. Then place the book in the True = Nonfiction box. (If your students are mature enough, you can also have them look at the spine label to check the type: letters only on fiction, nonfiction has numbers and letters.)

Check for Understanding

- Sing *Books are Great!*
- Select four books: two fiction and two obvious (photos of real animal) nonfiction, from the book display.
- Challenge students to look at the cover and point to the box that names the type of book.
- Call on students to come and place the books in the correct boxes.

Extension Activity: Frogs Hop Where?

Preparation

- Make a transparency of the action song, *Froggy Hop Parade* on page 52 for children to see and sing along.
- Make an obstacle course in the room for the kids to hop between, over, under, around, and beside.
- Bookmark the Web site, www.enchantedlearning.com/themes/frog.shtml.

  Optional: Copy the pattern or use construction paper to make or help students make the frog and toad patterns on pages 49-50.

Sharing the Lesson

- Explain that children will be using a song to tell where the frogs can hop.

- Read aloud each word on the transparency and tell the students they will participate in the *Froggy Hop Parade* to understand the meaning of these words.
- Say the word, *between,* and then sing the *Froggy Hop Parade* song on page 52 while demonstrating hopping between something in the obstacle course (Ex.: 2 chairs)
- Direct the children to get in line behind you and follow your movements as you announce each word, then sing and hop the meaning of that word until all the children have experienced it. Continue until all words are done. (Note: *forward* is another spatial word addressed in the song.)

Check for Understanding

- Go to the Web site, www.enchantedlearning.com/themes/frog.shtml and click on the *Five Little Speckled Frogs* in the *Frog Rhymes* box.
- View the rhyme, and then go back to the *Frog Rhymes* box to click on the *Online Coloring* page.
- Call on kids to name the colors so you can paint the picture. Each frog must be a different color.
- Use the item name and color in the picture. (Example: blue frog)
- Call on students to demonstrate and/or say the words that fill in the blanks below:

Pair 1: Over or Under

(Demonstrate arm movements for appropriate answers. Curve arm over head or under chin. Assess each student's understanding via arm movements.)

1. The _____ frog is over or under the dragonfly.
2. The dragonfly is over the _____ frog.

Pair 2: Behind or Between

(Demonstrate the meaning of *behind, beside,* and *between* prior to asking these questions.)

The big leaf is <u>behind</u> or <u>between</u> the little leaves?

The little leaves are <u>behind</u> or <u>beside</u> the big leaf?

Pair 3: Forward or Around

(This one is far more abstract.)

Challenge Question:

When we did the froggy hop, did we put our feet forward or around us?

Are the walls of our room around us or do they move us forward?

- Optional: use patterns on pages 49-50 for children to make a frog and/or toad puppet to take home after the frog lessons.

Recommended Bibliography

Fiction

Fine As We Are by Algy Craig Hall. Boxer Books, 2008.

Finklehopper Frog by Irene Livingston. Tricycle Press, 2003.

Frog and Toad are Friends by Arnold Lobel. HarperCollins, 1979.

A Frog in the Bog by Karma Wilson. Margaret K. McElderry Books, 2003.

A Frog Thing by Eric Drachman. Kidwick Books, 2006.

Jump, Frog, Jump! by Robert Kalan. HarperFestival, 2002.

One Frog Sang by Shirley Parenteau. Candlewick Press, 2007.

The Tale of Toad and Badger by Mary Jane Begin. Little, Brown and Company, 2008.

Yuck!! A Toad by Hilario. Hardenville S. A., 2006.

Nonfiction

Frog by Claire Llewellyn. NorthWood Press, 2003.

Frog by Lisa Magloff. DK Publishing, 2003.

Frog by Louise Spilsbury. Heinemann Library, 2005.

The Frog in the Pond by Dana Meachen Rau. Marshall Cavendish, 2007.

Hop Frog by Rick Chrustowski. Henry Holt & Company, 2003.

The Life Cycle of a Frog by Lisa Trumbauer. Pebble Books, 2002.

Pet Frog by Robin Nelson. Lerner Publishing Group, 2003.

Red-Eyed Tree Frog by Joy Cowley. Scholastic, 2006.

Toad by the Road: A Year in the Life of These Amazing Amphibians by Joanne Ryder. Henry Holt & Company, 2007.

Web Sites

Frogs and Toads in Color and Sound. www.naturesound.com/frogs/frogs.html. Twelve photographs are featured in this photo-album, along with RealAudio sound recordings of each species' calls.

Frogs and Toads at Enchanted Learning. www.enchantedlearning.com/themes/frog.shtml. Rhymes, crafts, quizzes, and printouts to color.

San Diego Zoo's Animal Bytes: Frog and Toad. www.sandiegozoo.org/animalbytes/t-frog_toad.html. Natural history and conservation information.

Frog Puppet Pattern

Fold one 9" x12" piece of green construction paper according to the pattern on this page to make a vertical column (in kid's terminology: a "hot dog bun"). Then fold the column in half widthwise. Fold each side of the half in half to meet the middle folded edge (column ends have openings). When you look at it and pull it apart slightly, it looks like the letter W.

Take the W and lay it on its side. One side has two folds, the other has one fold and two sets of open ends. Place your thumb inside one open end and your other fingers in the other open end. Move your hands to make the puppet talk. Decorate the "face" any way you wish.

Optional Puppet Pattern: If you have advanced students and/or a parent/student helper to assist, you may wish to copy the pattern page for each child and have them fold and color their own frog or toad. (You might use ¾" Avery label color coding dots to stick on for eyes. I buy a pack of yellow ones and cut them apart into sets of two for each child.)

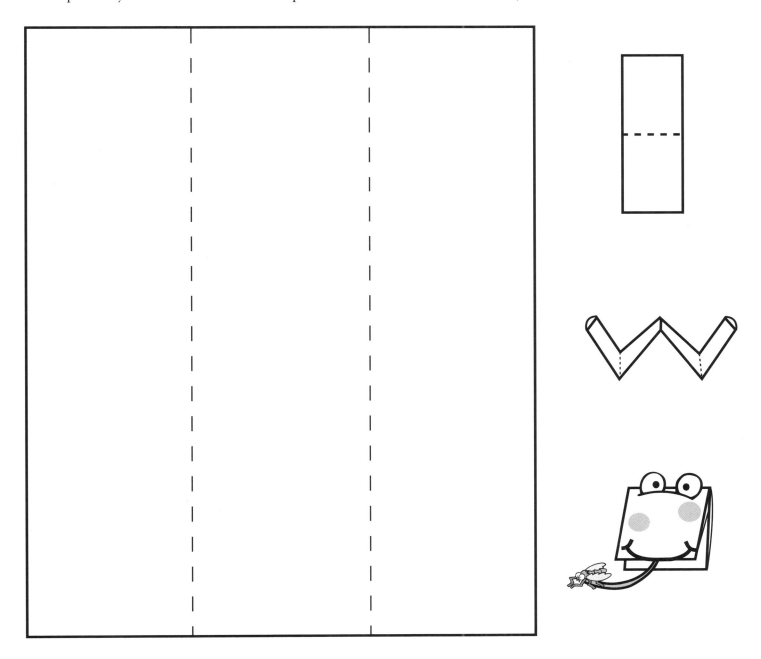

Toad Puppet Pattern

Using brown construction paper, follow the frog puppet directions on page 49.

Books Are Great!

(Use a deep froggy voice to sing to the tune of *Row, Row, Row Your Boat*.)

Sing a silly song of the frogs

in the Learning Pond.

Read-it! Read-it!

Read-it! Read-it!

Books are really fun!

Froggy Hop Parade

(Sung to the tune of *The Bunny Hop*.)

Put your frog feet bē-tween,
do the froggy hop,
Do the froggy hop
with a hop, hop, hop.

Put your frog feet over,
do the froggy hop,
Do the froggy hop
with a hop, hop, hop.

Put your frog feet under,
do the froggy hop,
Do the froggy hop
with a hop, hop, hop.

Put your frog feet around,
do the froggy hop,
Do the froggy hop
with a hop, hop, hop.

Put your frog feet bē-side,
do the froggy hop,
Do the froggy hop
with a hop, hop, hop.

Put your frog feet bē-hind,
do the froggy hop,
Do the froggy hop
with a hop, hop, hop.

Put your frog feet forward,
do the froggy hop,
Do the froggy hop
with a hop, hop, hop.

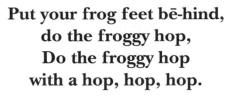

Farm Friends: Rhymes & Reasons

McRel Standards

Language Arts & Music

(Both listed in the Introduction on page 6.)

Agricultural Education—Agriculture in History & Society

- Understands the connections between agriculture and society

Science—Life Science

- Understands the relationships among organisms and their physical environments

Life Work

- Studies or pursues specific job interests

Theatre

- Uses acting skills

Lesson Objectives

- Listen for rhyming word patterns and respond with a rhyming word.
- Identify the purpose of farm animals and the products they provide.
- Use visual and auditory cues to dramatize a story with puppets.

Introduce the Lesson

Preparation

- Make the farmer man and farmer woman puppets using the pattern directions on pages 56–57.
- Make a transparency of the *Farm Animals* song on page 58 for students to see and sing along.

Presentation

- Display the transparency of the *Farm Animals* song.
- Use the farmer man and farmer woman puppets to sing *Farm Animals* on page 58.
- Call on students to name the farm animals and fill in the blanks under the animals' pictures.

Sharing the Story Lesson

Preparation

- Select and display a variety of fiction and nonfiction farm animals books.
- Optional: bookmark the Web site, www.dltk-teach.com/rhymes/five_little_chickens2.htm.

Presentation

- Ask students to listen to the song again and fill in the blanks with words that rhyme with sheep and eat. Remind them that rhyming words sound the same.
- Read one of the following rhyming books about the farm aloud: *Down on the Farm, Faraway Farm,* or *Farm Flu.*
- Select some of the rhyming word pairs used in the story. Say the first part of the rhyme and have the children finish it.

Check for Understanding

- Use the farmer man and farmer woman puppets to sing the *Animals Live on a Farm* song again.
- Ask students to finish these farm-themed rhyming word pairs with the names of animals from the transparency. Direct them

to listen for the sounds at the end of the words to make the match. Do one as an example.

1. Truck and D _ _ _ (*Duck*)
2. Big and P _ _ (*Pig*)
3. How and C _ _ (*Cow*)
4. Coat and G _ _ _ (*Goat*)
5. Keep and Sh _ _ _ (*Sheep*)

- Optional: go to the bookmarked Web site and share the *Five Little Chickens* rhyme with graphics. After each verse, say the first word that is part of a rhyming pair and ask students to tell you what it rhymes with. (Example: squirm and worm)

Extension Activity:
Farm Friends Operetta Puppet Show

Preparation

- Locate the transparency of the *Farm Animals* song.

- Select a nonfiction farm animal book with photos and text describing a variety of farm animals.

- Make the transparency of the *Farmyard Operetta* song on pages 59–60.

- Buy (stores, garage sales), borrow, or request donated puppets or make the farmyard animal stick puppets on pages 61–67.

Sharing the Lesson

- Use the farmer man and farmer woman puppets to sing the *Farm Animals* song.

- Picture read the nonfiction book.

- Explain to students that they will participate in a *Farmyard Operetta* puppet show to find out what each animal provides the farmer to sell for a living. Define the word, "operetta," as a short story sung in a song instead of read from a book.

1. Discuss and demonstrate appropriate puppetry etiquette. (See page 7 of the Introduction.)

- Display the transparency with the words to the *Farmyard Operetta* song.

- Sing the first verse of the *Farmyard Operetta* to demonstrate how the puppet will receive visual and auditory cues to say its sound. Students should listen for animal's name and raise their puppet high in the air while making its sound. As soon as it has finished its sound, it is brought down beside the student again.

- Name each animal and say the sound that will be made in the operetta.

- Choose students to help pass out puppets: chickens, cows, ducks, goats, pigs, sheep, and turkeys.

- Present the operetta, giving cues for each animal to participate by saying its sound three times at the end of each verse.

Check for Understanding

- Tell the children the animals must go back to the barn to rest.

- Tell them that each group of animals must wait to hear their sound and the food they provide, before they can be put in the barn.

- Make the sound of the animals and name the foods they provide.

- Assist the children as they place the animals back in the barn. (I use a separate plastic bin for each animal group's barn.)

Recommended Bibliography

Fiction

Clip-Clop by Nicola Smee. Boxer Books, 2006.

Down on the Farm by Merrily Kutner. Holiday House, 2004.

Faraway Farm by Ian Whybrow. Carolrhoda Books, 2006.

Farm Flu by Teresa Bateman. Albert Whitman, 2001.

How Many Kisses Do You Want Tonight? by Varsha Bajaj. Little, Brown and Company, 2004.

On the Farm by David Elliot. Candlewick Press, 2008.

Punk Farm by Jarrett Krosoczka. Knopf, 2005.

Punk Farm on Tour by Jarrett Krosoczka. Knopf, 2007.

Nonfiction

All Around the Farm (John Deere Series) by Heather Alexander. DK Publishing, 2007.

Animals on the Farm by Sue Barraclough. Raintree Steck-Vaughn, 2006.

Cut and Paste Farm Animals by Rosie Hankin. Gareth Stevens, 2007.

Fantastic Farm Machines by Cris Peterson. Boyds Mills Press, 2006.

Out and About at the Dairy Farm by Andy Murphy. Picture Window Books, 2003.

Who Grows Up on the Farm? A Book about Farm Animals and Their Offspring by Theresa Longenecker. Picture Window Books, 2003.

Web Sites

DLTK's Growing Together. www.dltk-teach.com/rhymes/five_little_chickens2.htm. Words for the "Five Little Chickens" rhyme.

Enchanted Learning. www.enchantedlearning.com. Do a keyword search for **farm**.

Farmer Man Puppet Pattern

Copy the pattern onto cardstock/tagboard. Then color, cut out, and glue it to the top of a paint stick to create a stick puppet. For durability, laminate before gluing.

Farmer Woman Puppet Pattern

Copy the pattern onto cardstock/tagboard. Then color, cut out, and glue it to the top of a paint stick to create a stick puppet. For durability, laminate before gluing.

Farm Animals

(Sung to the tune of *Mary Had a Little Lamb.*)

Cows and pigs and hens and sheep

Hens and sheep, hens and sheep

Cows and pigs and hens and sheep

Go to the barn to go to sleep.

Sheep and _ _ _ _ _

Animals make food to eat, food to eat, food to eat.

Animals make food to eat,

Healthy things are such a treat.

Eat and _ _ _ _ _

Farmland Operetta

(Sing the first three lines of each verse to the tune of *Row, Row, Row Your Boat.*)

Bok! Bok! Bok! I say, each and every day.
Eggs and meat will come from me
When people want to pay.
(Say sound.) Bok! Bok! Bok!

Moo! Moo! Moo! I say, each and every day.
Milk and meat will come from me
When people want to pay.
(Say sound.) Moo! Moo! Moo!

Quack! Quack! Quack! I say, each and every day.
Eggs and meat will come from me
When people want to pay.
(Say sound.) Quack! Quack! Quack!

Baaah! Baaah! Baaah! I say each and every day.
Milk and meat will come from me
When people want to pay.
(Say sound.) Baaah! Baaah! Baaah!

Oink! Oink! Oink! I say, each and every day.
Ham and bacon come from me
When people want to pay.
(Say sound.) Oink! Oink! Oink!

Baa! Baa! Baa! I say, each and every day,
Meat and wool will come from me
When people want to pay.
(Say sound.) Baa! Baa! Baa!

Gobble! Gobble! Gobble! I say, each and every day.
Eggs and meat will come from me
When people want to pay.
(Say sound.) Gobble! Gobble! Gobble!

Farm Animal Puppet Pattern: Chicken

Copy the pattern onto cardstock/tagboard. Then color, cut out, and glue it to the top of a paint stick to create a stick puppet. For durability, laminate before gluing.

Farm Animal Puppet Pattern: Cow

Copy the pattern onto cardstock/tagboard. Then color, cut out, and glue it to the top of a paint stick to create a stick puppet. For durability, laminate before gluing.

Farm Animal Puppet Pattern: Duck

Copy the pattern onto cardstock/tagboard. Then color, cut out, and glue it to the top of a paint stick to create a stick puppet. For durability, laminate before gluing.

Farm Animal Puppet Pattern: Goat

Copy the pattern onto cardstock/tagboard. Then color, cut out, and glue it to the top of a paint stick to create a stick puppet. For durability, laminate before gluing.

Farm Animal Puppet Pattern: Pig

Copy the pattern onto cardstock/tagboard. Then color, cut out, and glue it to the top of a paint stick to create a stick puppet. For durability, laminate before gluing.

Farm Animal Puppet Pattern: Sheep

Copy the pattern onto cardstock/tagboard. Then color, cut out, and glue it to the top of a paint stick to create a stick puppet. For durability, laminate before gluing.

Farm Animal Puppet Pattern: Turkey

Copy the pattern onto cardstock/tagboard. Then color, cut out, and glue it to the top of a paint stick to create a stick puppet. For durability, laminate before gluing.

Gardens Growing

McRel Standards

Language Arts & Music

(Both listed in the Introduction on page 6.)

Agricultural Education—Animal/Plant/Resource Handling

- Understands the essential elements of plant and animal care

Science

- Understands relationships among organisms and their physical environment

Thinking and Reasoning

- Effectively uses mental processes that are based on identifying similarities and differences

Lesson Objectives

- Dramatize via storytelling song the growth cycle from seed to plant.
- Identify the parts of a plant.
- Distinguish the basic needs for plant growth.
- Name plants and/or animals that harm, destro, and/or eat plants.

Introduce the Lesson:
Let's All Plant a Garden

Preparation

- Make a transparency from page 72 of the *Let's All Plant a Garden* song for students to see and sing along.

Presentation

- Display the song transparency from page 72, and direct the children to mimic your actions as you sing the song.

Let's All Plant a Garden

(Sing to the tune of *If You're Happy and You Know It* and demonstrate actions.)

Verse 1

(Action: Use whole body to dramatize digging a hole with a shovel.)

Let's all plant a garden, diggety-dig, dig-dig. (Repeat.)

Oh! Let's all plant a garden. Oh! Let's all plant a garden.

Oh! Let's all plant a garden, diggety-dig, dig-dig.

Verse 2

(Action: Bend over and drop seeds in pretend hole with hand.)

Let's drop some seeds down in the hole, ploppity-plop, plop-plop. (Repeat.)

Oh! Let's drop some seeds down in the hole. Oh! Let's drop some seeds down in the hole.

Oh! Let's drop some seeds down in the hole, ploppity-plop, plop-plop.

Verse 3

(Action: Use whole body to dramatize raking.)

Let's cover them with dirt, rakety-rake, rake-rake. (Repeat.)

Oh! Let's cover them with dirt. Oh! Let's cover them with dirt.

Oh! Let's cover them with dirt, rakety-rake, rake-rake.

Verse 4

*(Action: Direct students to watch as you cup your hands around your mouth and bend down to spray the seeds, by sticking out your tongue and blowing. As a side note, this is the kids' most favorite part, but it's very important that they aim at their feet/hole. They do the tongue blowing instead of saying words squirty-squirt. **Another option** is to simply have the kids panto-mime watering a garden saying, "Shh-shh-shh.")*

Let's spray them with water, squirty-squirt, squirt-squirt.

Oh! Let's spray them with water. Oh! Let's spray them with water.

Oh! Let's spray them with water, squirty-squirt, squirt-squirt.

Finish the song with these instructions:

Instruct the students to squat down into a tight ball like a seed in the ground. While squatting, tell them a seed is covered with a shell called a seed coat. Then demonstrate and have them perform the same motions as a growing plant: break out of the seed coat by pushing arms out from body, then push arms up through "dirt," and reach for the sun.

Sharing the Story Lesson

Preparation

- Select and display a variety of garden books.
- Optional: collect and add a variety of gardening tools to the book display.

Presentation

- Read aloud and discuss one of these fiction books.

  Pre-K: *The Carrot Seed.* A little boy plants and cares for a seed although his father, mother, and big brother tell him it will never grow. It does, and there's a huge carrot to prove it. This book lends itself to simple sequencing and a very basic 1, 2, 3 approach to teaching the growth cycle.

  Use the sequence cards on page 73 to have the children take turns coming up to put the cards in order: use ordinal number order of 1st, 2nd, 3rd, 4th, and 5th.

  K: *How Groundhog's Garden Grew.* Groundhog is causing problems by eating the produce from his neighbor's garden, so squirrel offers to teach him how to grow his own garden. This book provides a more in-depth description of the growth cycle, from instructions on how to collect and store the seeds until the weather is right for planting, to the actual harvesting of the produce. In addition to teaching garden-ing, it has multiple cross-curricular ties in social studies values: awareness of neigh-bors' feelings, teamwork, sharing the har-vest with others, etc.

- Picture read or read aloud a nonfiction book about gardens such as *From the Garden: A Counting Book about Growing Food* to rein-force the growth cycle concept.

- Select and read a poem a day from *Busy in the Garden: Poems* throughout the unit on the plant growth cycle.

Check for Understanding

- Use the transparency to sing the song again to reiterate the role of a gardener and the essential steps for growing plants.

- Challenge students to name the problem plant or animal in *The Carrot Seed* (weed) and *How Groundhog's Garden Grew* (ground-hog eating his neighbor's garden). Give clues as needed.

- Encourage students to check out garden books to picture read and read aloud with their families and friends.

Extension Activity:
Garden Friends and Foes

Preparation

- Locate the transparency of the *Let's All Plant a Garden* song.

- Make a transparency of the *Garden Friend or Foe?* Venn diagram on page 74.

Sharing the Story Lesson

- Review the basic needs of plants: soil, sunlight, and water. Record in left circle of Venn diagram.

- Explain that just because a garden is planted and the gardener provides for its basic needs, that doesn't guarantee that the garden will stay healthy and alive. In fact, sunlight and water actually belong in the center of the diagram, because too much of either or too little of either can kill a plant.

- Define the meaning of the word "foe" and ask children to listen to the story to see which plants or animals could be foes. Note which plants or animals are friendly to the child, but not necessarily good for the plants.

- Read *Animals in the Garden* or *Garden Friends aloud* and list plants or animals that can be beneficial or harmful, healthy or unhealthy predators to a garden. Record those answers in the appropriate circles of the Venn diagram.

- Challenge students to name other local foes that could harm or destroy a garden (insects, deer, rabbits, birds, dogs, etc.). Discuss and record those answers in the right circle.

  (Optional: A follow up picture read or read aloud of *Corduroy's Garden* depicts the dog digging up the seeds.)

Checking for Understanding

This is a higher level thinking activity since some of these animals are not listed in the books.

- Call on students to give a thumbs up if something is a friend to the garden, thumbs down if it is a foe to the garden, or thumbs to the side if they're not sure:

  1. Deer – unhealthy: eats leaves and produce
  2. Butterfly – healthy: spreads pollen
  3. Bird – healthy: eats insects/unhealthy: eats produce
  4. Rabbit – unhealthy: eats produce
  5. Squirrel – unhealthy: eats produce
  6. Honeybee – healthy: spreads pollen
  7. Grasshopper – unhealthy: eats holes in leaves
  8. Ant – unhealthy: eats produce
  9. Frog – healthy: eats insects
  10. Cutworm – unhealthy: eats plant leaves

- Discuss answers as needed and record in Venn diagram.

- Ask students to give rationale as to why the gardener is in the middle of the Venn diagram. (Can choose to protect garden to keep it healthy or leave garden unprotected and let foes harm or destroy it.)

Recommended Bibliography

Fiction

The Carrot Seed by Ruth Krauss. HarperCollins, 2005.

Corduroy's Garden by Alison Inches. Viking, 2002.

The Garden That We Grew by Joan Holub. Viking, 2001.

Grandma's Garden by Mercer Mayer. Gingham Dog Press, 2003.

How Groundhog's Garden Grew by Lynne Cherry. Blue Sky Press, 2003.

Nonfiction

Animals in the Garden by Elisabeth de Lambilly. Gareth Stevens, 2007.

Busy in the Garden by George Shannon. Greenwillow Books, 2006.

From Seed to Plant by Allan Fowler. Children's Press, 2001.

From the Garden by Michael Dahl. Picture Window Books, 2004.

Garden Friends edited by Elizabeth Hester. DK Publishing, 2003.

Plant Packages: A Book About Seeds by Susan Blackaby. Picture Window Books, 2003.

Tops and Bottoms by Janet Stevens. Scholastic, 1996.

Web Sites

DLTK's Learn About Flowers Craft. www.dltk-holidays.com/spring/mflower.html. Printable pattern and instructions to "build" a potted plant.

Preschool Education Science: Garden. www.preschooleducation.com/scgarden.shtml. Simple instructions for rooting and growing vegetables and plants.

Let's All Plant a Garden

by Aileen Kirkham, ©2007
(Sung to the tune of *If You're Happy and You Know It.*)

Let's all plant a garden, diggety-dig, dig-dig. (Repeat.)
Oh! Let's all plant a garden. Oh! Let's all plant a garden.
Oh! Let's all plant a garden, diggety-dig, dig-dig.

Let's drop some seeds down in the hole, ploppity-plop,
plop-plop. (Repeat.)
Oh! Let's drop some seeds down in the hole.
Oh! Let's drop some seeds down in the hole.
Oh! Let's drop some seeds down in the hole,
ploppity-plop, plop-plop.

Let's cover them with dirt, rakety-rake, rake-rake. (Repeat.)
Oh! Let's cover them with dirt. Oh! Let's cover them with dirt.
Oh! Let's cover them with dirt, rakety-rake, rake-rake.

Let's spray them with water, squirty-squirt, squirt-squirt.
(Repeat.)
Oh! Let's spray them with water.
Oh! Let's spray them with water.
Oh! Let's spray them with water, squirty-squirt, squirt-squirt.

Story Sequence Cards

Have children take turns putting theses cards in order.

Garden Friend or Foe? Venn Diagram

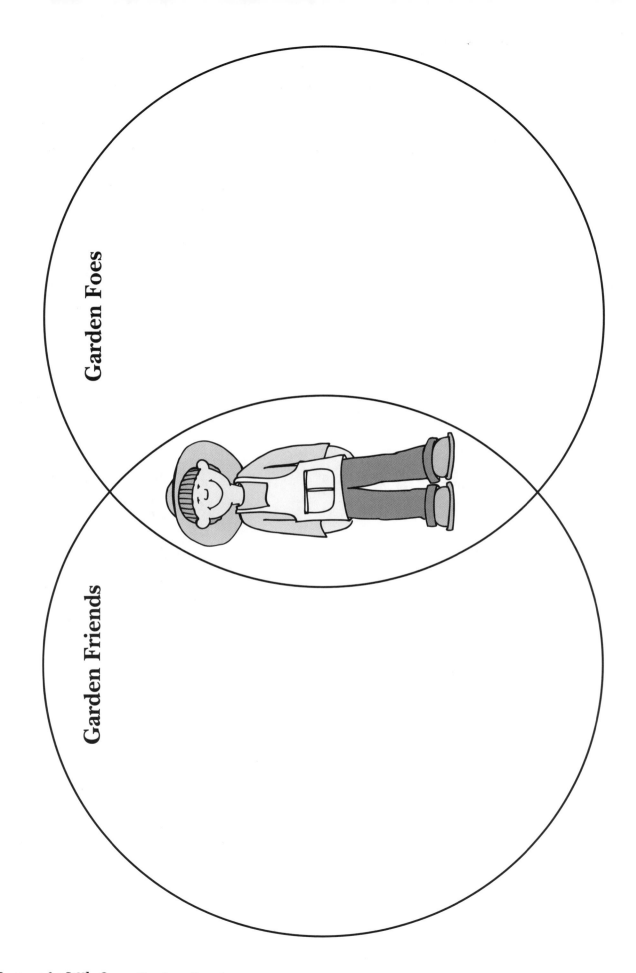

Garden Foes

Garden Friends

Gobblin' Good Books:
Harvesting the Love of Literature

Note: Must be taught in October for bulletin board display in November.

McRel Standards

Language Arts & Music

(Both listed in the Introduction on page 6.)

Science—Life Science

- Understands relationships among organisms and their physical environment

Lesson Objectives

- Participate in a motivational reading program to reinforce the importance of reading in the library, classroom, and/or at home.

- Read or listen to 10 books read aloud in the library, classroom, and/or at home.

- Explore the season of fall.

- Have an adult to record the titles on the Gobblin' Good Books Reading Record.

- Return the sheet to class or library by November first.

Introduce the Lesson:
Gobblin' Good Books

Preparation

- Make a turkey stick puppet according to the pattern on page 67.

- Make transparency of the Gobblin' Good Books Reading Record found on page 78.

Note:

Because one of my kindergarten teachers sometimes found it hard to get all the record sheets back once she'd sent them home, she suggested that I make every kindergarten teacher a master copy of the Gobblin' Good Books Reading Record Sheet (see Gobblin' Good Books Reading Record on page 78 for reference). The master copy should already list the titles I would be reading aloud to the students, and remaining turkey feathers could then be used by the teachers for the titles they read to their classes. When all the feathers were filled out on the master copy, it could then be copied and distributed to every child to color. Every reading record, classroom or personal, could then be put on display on a November bulletin board.

Presentation

- Use the turkey stick puppet to talk to the kids to define the meaning of Gobblin' Good Books. (Books are like the corn that a turkey eats to grow, we need to "gobble" them up for brain food. Tease by asking kids if we really eat the books. Use this opportunity to remind them about book care.)

- Display the transparency with the turkey graphic and song.

- Sing the song on the record sheet and demonstrate the actions named in the song *Gobblin' Good Books* on page 79.

Sharing the Story Lesson

Preparation

- Select and display a variety of fall-themed books: fall leaves, scarecrows, and squirrels.

Presentation

- Picture read a nonfiction book and read it aloud. (My recommended favorites are *The Squirrel, The Busy Little Squirrel* and *Nuts to You!*)

- Discuss a squirrel's need to store food for the winter.
- Make the analogy that kids' brains need to store words and pictures to make them better learners.

Check for Understanding

- Use the transparency to sing the song again to reiterate the purpose of the Gobblin' Good Books reading program.
- Ask the children what needs to be written on each turkey feather.
- Ask them why there's a need to read and hear good books.
- Tell the children that the library wants to honor them for participating in the Gobblin' Good Books program by displaying their reading records on a bulletin board in the library/classroom for everyone to see.
- Display reading records. If you back the record sheet with a piece of construction paper it will make the bulletin board display much nicer.

Extension Activity: Spring into Reading

Eggstra Special Read-Alouds! A Basketful of Books

Use the same school/home literacy program format as listed for Gobblin' Good Books, but use spring book selections to introduce the Eggstra Special Read-Alouds Record Sheet and song found on pages 80–81. Record book titles on the eggs.

Recommended Bibliography

Fiction

The Busy Little Squirrel by Nancy Tafuri. Simon & Schuster, 2007.

Earl the Squirrel by Don Freeman. Viking, 2005.

In the Leaves by Huy Voun Lee. Henry Holt & Company, 2005.

It's Fall by Linda Glaser. Millbrook Press, 2001.

Jeb Scarecrow's Pumpkin Patch by Jana Dillon. Houghton Mifflin, 1992.

Leaf Man by Lois Ehlert. Harcourt, 2005.

Leaves by David Ezra Stein. Putnam, 2007.

Leaves! Leaves! Leaves! by Nancy Elizabeth Wallace. Marshall Cavendish, 2007.

The Little Scarecrow Boy by Margaret Wise Brown. HarperCollins, 1998.

The Lonely Scarecrow by Tim Preston. Dutton Children's Books, 1999.

Now It's Fall by Lois Lenski. Random House, 2005.

Nuts by Paula Gerritsen. Front Street, 2006.

Nuts to You! by Lois Ehlert. Voyager Books, 2004.

Ouch! by Ragnhild Scamell. Good Books, 2006.

Red Leaf, Yellow Leaf by Lois Ehlert. Harcourt Brace, 1991.

The Scarecrow's Hat by Ken Brown. Andersen, 2002.

Scaredy Squirrel by Mèlanie Watt. Kids Can Press, 2006.

Who Loves the Fall? by Bob Raczka. Albert Whitman, 2007.

Nonfiction

Animals in the Fall by Martha E. H. Rustad. Capstone Press, 2008.

Birds in Fall by Stephen Maslowski. Smart Apple Media, 2002.

Leaves by Vijaya Bodach. Capstone Press, 2007.

Leaves in Fall by Martha E. H. Rustad. Capstone Press, 2008.

The Squirrel by James V. Bradley. Chelsea House Publishers, 2006.

Squirrels and Their Nests by Martha E. H. Rustad. Capstone Press, 2008.

People in Fall by Martha E. H. Rustad. Capstone Press, 2008.

Web Sites

Autumn Printables.
www.dltkholidays.com/fall/printables.htm.
Print out Awards and Certificates, Bingo Cards, Bookmarks, Calendars, Chore Charts, Coupons, Dominos, Doorknob Holders, Gift Tags, Greeting Cards, Memory Cards, Money Cards, Recipe Cards, Treat Bags, Worksheets, and Writing Paper: Customizable or Standard.

DLTK's Growing Together.
www.dltk-teach.com.
Do keyword searches for *fall leaves, scarecrow,* and/or *squirrel* to get a multitude of ideas and other recommended Web sites.

National Geographic.
animals.nationalgeographic.com/animals/ mammals/squirrel.html. Natural history information and multimedia resources.

Oriental Trading.
www.orientaltrading.com. Order craft supplies, including feathers.

Gobblin' Good Books Reading Record

Follow these steps:

1. Sing the Gobblin' Good Books song daily before the read-aloud.
2. Read the book aloud and talk about your favorite parts, and how it relates to what you're learning in school.
3. Write the title of the book on a turkey tail feather.
4. Continue this daily read aloud until all 10 feathers are filled in with book titles.
5. Return this record sheet to the classroom/library by November 1 for display.

Child's Name _____   Teacher's Name _____

GOBBLIN' GOOD BOOKS

(Sing to the tune of the *Hokey Pokey* and act out the words.)

You check a good book out,
You get ready to read
With your friends at school
Or your family at home,

You share the pictures on the pages and
You read words, too.
Books are gobblin' good for you!

Gobble, gobble, good books,
Gobble, gobble, good books,
Reading's what it's all about, YEAH!

Eggstra Special Read-Alouds Record Sheet

Follow these steps:

1. Sing the *Crack'em Open and Read* song daily before the read aloud.
2. Read the book aloud and talk about your favorite parts, and how it relates to what you're learning in school.
3. Write the title of the book on an egg.
4. Continue this daily read-aloud until all 10 eggs are filled in with book titles.
5. Return this record sheet to the classroom/library by _____ (date) for display.

Child's Name _____   **Teacher's Name** _____

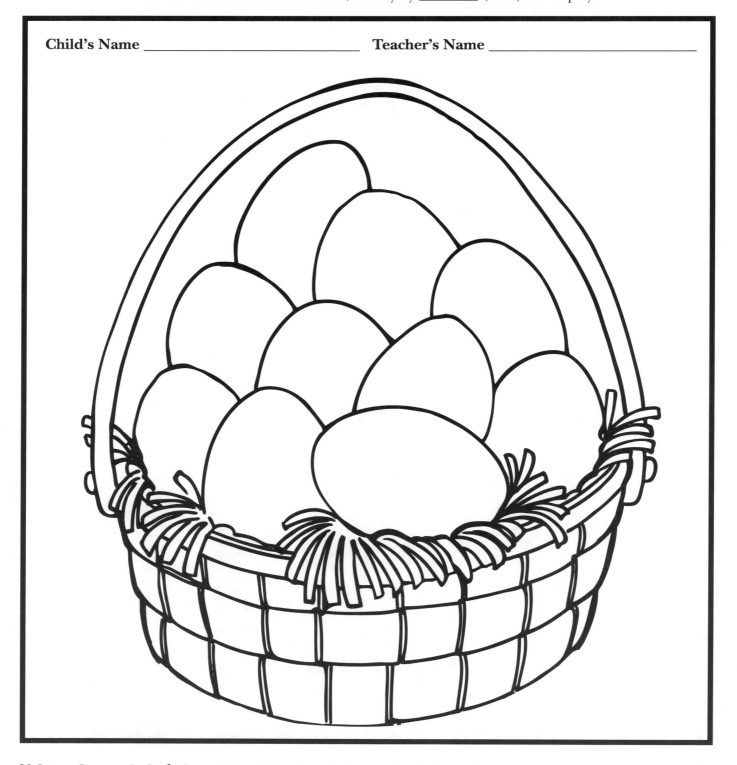

Crack 'Em Open And Read!

(Sing to the tune of the *Hokey Pokey* and act out the words.)

You check a good book out; you get
ready to read
with your friends at school
Or with family at home.
You share the pictures on the pages and
You read words, too.
Books are eggstra fun for you!
Crack'em open and read,
Crack'em open and read.
Reading's what it's all about, YEAH!

Habitats x 2: Desert & Rainforest

McRel Standards

Language Arts & Music

(Both listed in the Introduction on page 6.)

Geography: Physical Systems

- Understands the characteristics of ecosystems on the earth's surface

Geography: Environment and Society

- Understands how physical systems affect human systems

Life Sciences

- Understands relationships among organisms and their physical environment

Thinking and Reasoning

- Effectively uses mental processes that are based on identifying similarities and differences

Lesson Objectives

- Understand that the desert and the rainforest habitats provide the three basic needs for life: food, water, and shelter.
- Observe attributes of flora and fauna in the desert and rainforest.
- Define a habitat as a community providing resources for humans and other animals.

Introduce the Lesson: Habitat Defined

Preparation

- Select and display an assortment of fiction and nonfiction books about deserts, rainforests, and the type of habitat in which your school is located (Example: woodlands).

- Bookmark Web sites (see bibliography in this section for recommended sites).
- Optional: use the horned toad puppet pattern on page 85 or choose a desert animal puppet to sing the *Habitat Song*.

Note: A horned toad is a type of lizard.

Presentation

- Use a desert animal puppet to sing:

  Habitat Song

  (Sung to the tune of the refrain in *Over in the Meadow.*)

  A desert is a habitat for many animals who need to live in a community just like me and you.

- Display a picture of a desert scene from a nonfiction book such as *Cactus Hotel* or from www.worldwildlife.org/wildplaces/cd/photos.cfm.

- Discuss the fact that a desert is a habitat that looks nearly lifeless, but many animals live there. The desert provides the three necessities of life: food, water, and shelter.

Sharing the Story Lesson

Preparation

- Have chart paper or a marker board on hand to record answers.

Presentation

- Read *Way Out in the Desert* aloud. Each time you finish reading/singing the text on the page, sing or say the habitat song to reinforce the meaning of the desert as a habitat. Alternate read aloud: *The Seed and the Giant Saguaro.*

- Discuss the type of animal on the page and what the text says about it.

- Explain that the place where the children live is their habitat, and that provides them with the three necessities of life, just as the desert animals' habitat does.

- Write down the three basic needs and ask the kids to share how their basic needs are met within their own community habitat. Record the childrens' answers. Examples:

    1. Food – grocery stores, gardens, restaurants, etc.

    2. Water – faucets, sprinkler, water fountains, etc.

    3. Shelter – apartments, house trailers, houses, etc.

Check for Understanding

- Use the transparency on page 86 to sing the *Habitat Song* again to reinforce the concept that a desert is a type of habitat.

- Challenge students to

    1. List the three basic necessities of a habitat.

    2. Name the type of habitat that looks lifeless, but isn't.

    3. Name the type of habitat they live in.

Extension Activity:
Habitat Comparisons–Desert vs. Rainforest

Preparation

- Make a transparency of the habitat comparison chart on page 87.

Presentation

- Challenge students to be rainforest scientists to watch (use hands to mimic binoculars), listen (use hands to cup ears to capture sound), and discover that a desert and rainforest have many attributes that are opposites.

- Read a picture book aloud, such as *The Rainforest Grew All Around* or *Over in the Jungle: a Rainforest Rhyme* that showcases plant and animal life found in the rainforest.

- Ask your rainforest scientists (students) to share their observations about the differences between a desert and a rainforest habitat in terms of rain, temperature, plant, and animal life. (Temperature is hot in both, but can be very cold in desert, share this observation if they don't have that background knowledge.)

- Record their observations on the habitat comparisons chart.

Check for Understanding

- Direct students to name the two groups of living things found in a desert and a rainforest: plants and animals. (Give clues as needed and/or refer to the completed comparison chart.)

- Call on students to remember the story's words AND pictures to name:

    1. One animal from the desert book not found in the rainforest. (Coyote)

    2. One animal from the rainforest book not found in the desert. (Sloth)

    3. One plant from the desert book not found in the rainforest. (Cactus)

    4. One plant from the rainforest not found in the desert. (Kapok tree)

- Add this data to the habitat comparison chart.

- Optional: Open the Web site, www.every-thingpreschool.com/themes/rainforest/songs.htm, then:

    1. Sing the song, *Layers in the Rainforest.*

    2. Call on students to come up a few at a time and build a human rainforest:

Emergent – standing on chairs

Canopy – kids standing on the floor in front of the chairs

Understory – kids kneeling on the floor in front of kids standing

Forest Floor – kids lying on the floor in front of kids kneeling.

Recommended Bibliography

Fiction

Over in the Jungle: A Rainforest Rhyme by Marianne Berkes. Dawn Publications, 2007.

The Seed and the Giant Saguaro by Jennifer Ward. Rising Moon, 2003.

Stone Pizza by Susan K. Mitchell. RGU Group, 2007. Desert animals serve as the main characters in this adaptation of the old tale, *Stone Soup*.

The Rainforest Grew All Around by Susan K. Mitchell. Sylvan Dell Publishing, 2007.

The Three Little Javelinas by Susan Lowell. Rising Moon, 1992.

Way Out in the Desert by T. J. Marsh and Jennifer Ward. Rising Moon, 1998.

Nonfiction

About Habitats: Deserts by Cathryn Sill. Peachtree Publishers, 2007.

Animal Babies in Rain Forests by Jennifer Schofield. Kingfisher, 2004.

Cactus Hotel by Brenda Z. Guiberson. Henry Holt & Company, 1991.

Coyote Steals the Blanket: An Ute Tale by Janet Stevens. Holiday House, 1993.

The Desert Alphabet Book by Jerry Pallotta. Charlesbridge,1994.

If I Ran the Rainforest by Bonnie Worth. Random House, 2003.

Life in a Desert by Carol K. Lindeen. Capstone Press, 2004.

Living in a Rainforest by Patty Whitehouse. Rourke Publishing, 2007.

Web Sites

Biome/Habitat Animal Printouts— Enchanted Learning. www.enchantedlearning.com/biomes. Biome information, charts, and puzzles.

DLTK's Animal Crafts for Kids. www.dltk-kids.com/animals/index.html. Animal crafts, coloring, printables, worksheets, and games.

Everything Preschool: Preschool Rain Forest Songs and Music. www.everythingpreschool.com/themes/rainforest/songs.htm. Lyrics to *Layers in the Rainforest*.

WF Chihuahuan Desert Photo Gallery. www.worldwildlife.org/wildplaces/cd/photos.cfm. An article about protecting the balance of a desert.

Horned Toad/Lizard Puppet Pattern

Copy the pattern onto cardstock/tagboard. Then color, cut out, and glue it to the top of a paint stick to create a stick puppet. For durability, laminate before gluing.

Habitat Song

(Sung to the tune of the refrain in *Over in the Meadow.*)

A desert is a habitat for many animals who need to live in a community just like me and you.

Habitat Comparison Chart

Record the attributes of a desert and a rainforest.

Desert	Rainforest

Insects vs. Spiders: Got Food?

McRel Standards

Language Arts & Music

(Both listed in the Introduction on page 6.)

Mathematics

- Uses and applies basic and advanced properties of the concept of numbers

Science—Life Science

- Understands the relationships among organisms and their physical environment

Lesson Objectives

- Use scientific observation and mathematical number concepts to differentiate between insects and spiders.
- Explore eating habits of insects and spiders.
- Define the predator and prey role of insects and spiders in the food chain.
- Sequence characters in a story.

Introduce the Lesson

Preparation

- Make a transparency of the song, *I Know an Old Lady Who Swallowed a Fly: Uh! Oh! Where Did It Go?* on page 92. This version is shorter to accomodate little ones' attention spans.
- Make the old lady sack puppet from the pattern on page 93.
- Photocopy page 94 with the patterns of the fly, spider, and bird onto cardstock.
- Write the words "Predator" and "Prey" on the board.

Presentation

- Display the transparency of the song and the old lady sack puppet with fly, spider, and bird pieces.
- Challenge the kids to listen carefully as you sing the song *I Know an Old Lady Who Swallowed a Fly: Uh! Oh! Where Did It Go?* from page 92 to see what creature was supposed to catch the preceding creature when the old lady ate them.
- Sing the song and make eating noises as you drop each creature in.
- Call on students to name the catchers in sequence and what they would eat:

  (Old lady—fly; spider—fly; bird—spider)

- Define the words "predator" and "prey," and explain how the concept was used in the story.
- Assess their understanding of the real world by asking; which predator/prey relationship shared in the story doesn't really happen except in a storybook?

Sharing the Story Lesson

Preparation

- Locate the story pattern pieces of the fly and the spider.
- Locate the book, *Miss Spider's Tea Party*.
- Select and display an assortment of fiction and nonfiction books about insects and spiders.

Presentation

- Hold up the fly and the spider pieces and ask the kids to look at them carefully.

- Tell the kids to count the legs to see which one has the most and which one has the least.

- Name the creatures and ask the kids to hold up fingers to show how many legs each creature has. Fly = six fingers for six legs, Spider = eight fingers for eight legs.

- Explain that the fly belongs to a large group of creatures know as insects and that all of them have six legs. Tell the kids that they can easily classify the difference between spiders and insects by counting the creatures' legs.

- Say this rhyme and have the kids echo each line to repeat it with you:

    Insects count to six,
    Spiders count to eight.
    Look carefully and see,
    Counting works just great!

- Read *Miss Spider's Tea Party* aloud.

Check for Understanding

- Ask the students why the insects didn't want to attend *Miss Spider's Tea Party.*

- Review the definitions of "predator" and "prey" as the basis for the author writing this story.

- Call on students to hold up their fingers to show how many legs insects like a fly have (six), and how many legs a spider has (eight).

- Echo say the rhyme:

    Insects count to six,
    Spiders count to eight.
    Look carefully and see,
    Counting works just great!

Extension Activity: Bugalicious!

Preparation

- Go to www.uky.edu/Ag/Entomology/yth-facts/bugfun/trivia.htm, and click on "Bug Food!" Click on "Bugfood I: Insect-themed Food."

    Print out a recipe of you choice. *Ants on a Log* would fit with the poem and the story. If kids are allergic to peanut butter, you could use pimento cheese spread and call it, *Ants* in *a Log*, with the pimentos being the red ants in the cheese. No raisins would be needed for this version. If kids don't like celery, put it on a cracker. (Caution: Celery strings may pose a choking hazard to young children.))

- Request ingredient donations for your chosen recipe from parents, or purchase them yourself.

- Acquire paper plates for serving.

- Make the ant puppet on page 95, or borrow or buy an ant puppet.

- Get 8½" x 11" manilla paper or another type of inexpensive drawing paper and fold each sheet in half so there are enough folded sheets for one per child.

Sharing the Story Lesson

- Ask the kids to guess if the poem and/or the story today will be about an insect or a spider. Give them this clue: the main character has six legs.

- Act out this edible insect poem. Hold the paint stick ant puppet behind your back until the last line, then let it crawl out from behind your back, and pretend to catch it with your mouth and eat it.

Ode to Ant-icipation
by Aileen Kirkham, 2008

I wish I had a yummy ant
to swallow down this day.

I've looked all over my backyard,
but guess it crawled away.

Just wait until tomorrow
for breakfast or for lunch.

I'll be sure to catch one then
and muncha, muncha, munch!

Optional: Read aloud, *Beetle McGrady Eats Bugs!* (De"bite"ful story!)

- Tell the kids they will be making an insect snack to eat today.

- Tell the kids that while they are waiting for their turn to make their snack, they will get to make a snack placemat.

- Direct them to draw a picture of an insect on one side of their paper and a spider on the other.

- Show them an example of how the fold is the dividing line for the pictures.

- Explain the directions for making the snack.

- Pass out drawing paper, one sheet folded in half for each child.

- Call them up a few at a time to make their snack a few at a time. (Involve parent helpers if possible.)

- Tell them to wait to eat until everyone has made a snack and put it on his or her placemat. At that time, you will give them permission to "catch those ants" and eat them.

Check for Understanding

- Call on students to hold up their fingers to show how many legs each creature has when you call out its name:

1. Insects like a fly: six
2. Spider: eight

- Echo say this rhyme:

Insects count to six,
Spiders count to eight.
Look carefully and see,
Counting works just great!

Recommended Bibliography

Fiction

Aaaarrgghh! Spider! by Lydia Monks. Houghton Mifflin, 2007.

Beetle McGrady Eats Bugs! by Megan McDonald. Greenwillow Books, 2005.

Bugs in My Hair?! by Catherine Stier. Albert Whitman, 2008. (Lice problem.)

Bow-Wow Bugs a Bug by Mark Newgarden and Megan Montague Cash. Harcourt, 2007.

Bumble Bugs and Elephants: A Big and Little Book by Margaret Wise Brown. HarperCollins, 2006. (Concept book about opposites.)

Diary of a Fly by Doreen Cronin. Joanna Cotler Books, 2007.

Diary of a Spider by Doreen Cronin. Joanna Cotler Books, 2005.

The Grouchy Ladybug by Eric Carle. HarperCollins, 1996.

The Honeybee and the Robber: A Moving/Picture Book by Eric Carle. Philomel Books, 2000. (Pop-up and pull tabs.)

How Many Bugs in a Box? A Pop-up Counting Book by David A. Carter. Simon & Schuster, 2006.

Itsy Bitsy, the Smart Spider by Charise Mericle Harper. Dial Books, 2004.

The Leaf Men and the Brave Good Bugs by William Joyce. HarperCollins, 2001.

Miss Spider's Tea Party by David Kirk. Scholastic, 1997.

Sophie's Masterpiece: A Spider's Tale by Eileen Spinelli. Aladdin, 2004.

The Very Busy Spider by Eric Carle. Hamish Hamilton, 1996.

The Very Clumsy Click Beetle by Eric Carle. Philomel Books, 1999. (Battery-operated sounds.)

The Very Hungry Caterpillar by Eric Carle. Puffin, 2003.

The Very Lonely Firefly by Eric Carle. Penguin Putnam, 2000. (Board book with a battery-operated page that lights up.)

The Very Quiet Cricket by Eric Carle. Philomel Books, 1997. (Battery operated sounds at end of the book.)

Nonfiction

About Insects: A Guide for Children by Cathryn Sill. Peachtree Publishers, 2003.

Alphabet of Insects by Barbie Heit Schwaeber. Soundprints, 2007. (CD and poster included.)

Are You a Spider? by Judy Allen. Kingfisher, 2003.

Backyard Bugs (series) from Picture Window Books, 2006.

Bugs by Monica Hughes. Bearport Publishing, 2006.

Bugs Are Insects by Anne Rockwell. HarperCollins, 2001.

Bugs for Lunch by Margery Facklam. Charlesbridge, 1999.

Bugs: Poems about Creeping Things by David L. Harrison. Wordsong, 2007.

Creepy, Crawly Baby Bugs by Sandra Markle. Walker & Co., 2003.

Drawing and Learning about Bugs: Using Shapes and Lines by Amy Bailey Muehlenhardt. Picture Window Books, 2004.

The Eensy-Weensy Spider by Mary Ann Hoberman. Little, Brown and Company, 2004.

The Eentsy, Weentsy Spider: Fingerplays and Action Rhymes by Joanna Cole and Stephanie Calmenson. Mulberry Books, 1991.

Giant Pop-Out Bugs: A Pop-Out Surprise Book. Chronicle Books, 2008.

It's a Good Thing There Are Insects by Allan Fowler. Children's Press, 2001.

Pattern Bugs by Trudy Harris. Millbrook Press, 2001.

The Spectacular Spider Book by Valerie Davies. School Specialty Pub., 2006.

Professional Books

Bugs by Jennifer Overend Prior. Teacher Created Materials, 1999.

Bugs, Bugs, Bugs! by Pamela Byrne Schiller. Gryphon House, 2006. (CD included.)

Theme-a-saurus: Bugs and Creepy Crawlers by Marsha Elyn Wright. Frank Schaffer Publications, 2004.

Web Sites

DLTK Growing Together. www.dltk-kids.com/crafts/insects. Insect crafts, coloring, printables, worksheets, and games.

Pestworld for Kids. www.pestworldforkids.org/home.asp. This site explores pest ecology as the intersection between human-created habitats and animal needs for food and shelter. It is designed for students and teachers in the elementary and middle school grades. The web site offers information resources, interactive learning games, science fair kits, and lesson plans that support national standards developed by the National Science Teacher Association and the National Council of Teachers of English.

University of Kentucky Entomology for Kids. www.ca.uky.edu/entomology/dept/youth.asp. This site is a gold mine of insect information from experts who have taken the time to make it teachable for all ages.

Yahoo! Kids. kids.yahoo.com/animals/insects. Natural history information about insects, including names and types.

I Know an Old Lady Who Swallowed a Fly: Uh! Oh! Where Did it Go?

(Same tune as original song.)

I know an old lady who swallowed a fly, I don't know why she swallowed a fly. Perhaps she'll die.
Uh! Oh! Where did it go?

I know an old lady who swallowed a spider that wiggled and jiggled and tickled inside her. She swallowed the spider to catch the fly. I don't know why she swallowed that fly. Perhaps she'll die.
Uh! Oh! Where did it go?

I know an old lady who swallowed a bird, a mockingbird whose song she'd heard. She swallowed the mockingbird to catch the spider that wiggled and jiggled and tickled inside her. She swallowed the spider to catch the fly. I don't know why she swallowed that fly. Perhaps she'll die.
Uh! Oh! Where did it go?

Old Lady Sack Puppet Face Pattern

Copy, color, and cut out face pattern. Laminate, if desired, and glue so top of head touches the top of a large brown paper grocery bag. Use scissors to cut through both the paper and paper bag layers of the middle of the mouth opening. Cut out the entire mouth area to make it large enough for the creatures to be dropped inside.

Cut an oval hole for the stomach close to the bottom of the bag. Use plastic wrap or a clean transparency sheet to tape to the inside of the bag over the stomach hole so the kids can see the creatures as they drop down in the tummy.

Example:

Fly, Spider, and Bird Piece Patterns

Copy the patterns onto cardstock/tagboard. Then color, cut out, and laminate for durability.

Hold up or display fly and spider pieces so children can use scientific observation and mathematical computation to count the number of legs.

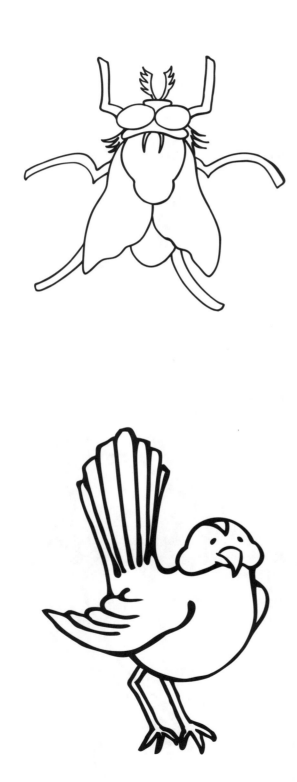

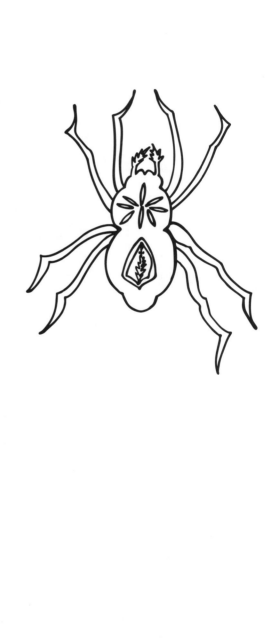

Ant Puppet Pattern

Copy the pattern onto cardstock/tagboard. Then color, cut out, and glue it to the top of a paint stick to create a stick puppet. For durability, laminate before gluing.

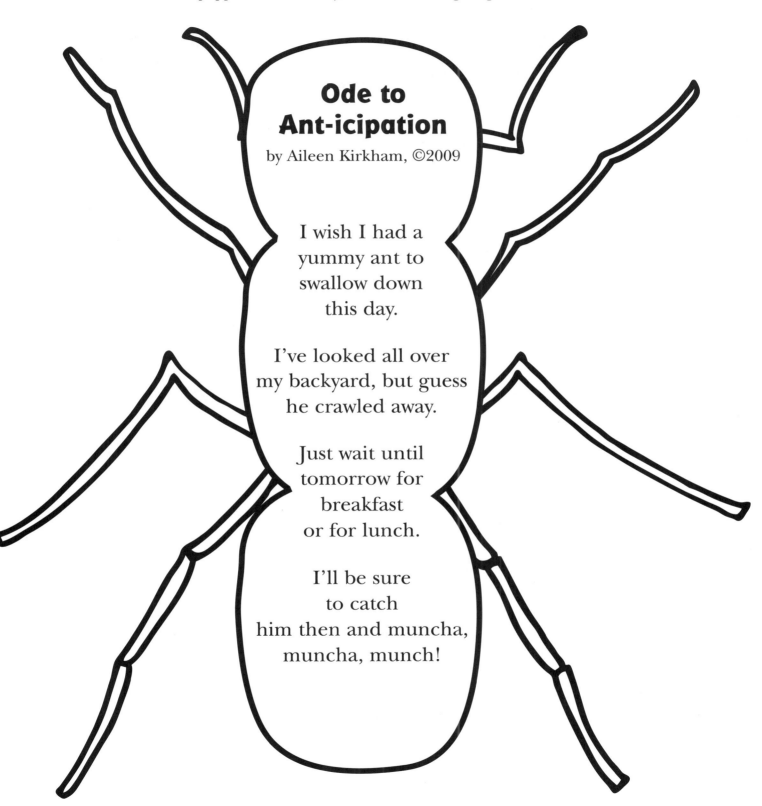

Ode to Ant-icipation
by Aileen Kirkham, ©2009

I wish I had a
yummy ant to
swallow down
this day.

I've looked all over
my backyard, but guess
he crawled away.

Just wait until
tomorrow for
breakfast
or for lunch.

I'll be sure
to catch
him then and muncha,
muncha, munch!

Monstrous Math: Feelings Count

McRel Standards

Language Arts & Music

(Both listed in the Introduction on page 6.)

Behavorial Studies

- Understands that group and cultural differences contribute to human development, identity, and behavior

- Understands conflict, cooperation, and interdependence among individuals, groups, and institutions

Mathematics

- Understands and applies basic and advanced properties of the concepts of numbers

- Uses basic and advanced procedures while performing the processes of computation

Theatre

- Uses acting skills

Thinking and Reasoning

- Understands and applies basic principles of logic and reasoning

Lesson Objectives

- Use mathematical computation.

- Use auditory and visual clues to make a one-to-one correspondence with ordinal numbers.

- Use comprehension skills to solve word problems.

- Participate in mathematical functions: addition and subtraction.

- Classify feelings: positive and negative.

- Explore options for conflict resolution.

Introduce the Lesson

Preparation

- Make a transparency from page 99 of the *Marching Monster Race* song for students to see and sing along.

Presentation

- Display the transparency of the *Marching Monster Race* song.

- Direct children to stand up and march as you sing the song *Marching Monster Race* from page 99 and mimic your facial expressions to show monster feelings.

  Have kids stand and march in place as they echo sing line two and hum lines three and four. Tell them to copy your facial expressions, too. If you don't know this tune, go to kids.niehs.nih.gov/lyrics for the melody.)

- Call on students to answer the question in the last line of the sentence.

- If need be, use the deductive process to cancel out numbers, until the winner is named. (Ex: Could 6 win, song words say no, could 9 win …)

- If group is mature enough, add the ordinal number to match with the number:

  Who came in first? One came in first and won! Who came in last? 10 came in 10th.

Sharing the Story Lesson

Preparation

- Select and display a variety of monster books: fiction and nonfiction.

- Make sure to include one of these three "count down" books: *Monster Countdown,*

Monster Math, or *Monster Musical Chairs* (this one allows you to play musical chairs in the story).

- Optional: Monster Mummy Wrap Game. Provide one roll of toilet paper for every four children.

Presentation

- Read one of the recommended "count down" books aloud.

- Play musical chairs and after each verse, recite the "count down" math statement. (Ex: We had 10, now we have nine.) Depending on the kids' developmental stage, you may need to play with only 10 kids at a time while the others watch, since counting back from numbers beyond 10 may be too hard. In other words, in a class of 22, you can't have a chair for everyone to play the first time if you're counting down from 10.

Checking for Understanding

- Challenge students to show their fingers as you orally count up and count down.

- Assess and correct as needed.

- Optional: Have kids play the Monster Mummy Wrap Game. Locate directions at www.4to40.com/games/print.asp?gid=25 Play it with groups to see who comes in 1ˢᵗ, 2ⁿᵈ, 3ʳᵈ, 4ᵗʰ, 5ᵗʰ, etc. Use the ordinal number names to proclaim winners.

Extension Activity: Monstrous Feelings

Preparation

- Locate the *Marching Monsters Race* song transparency.

- Locate the book, *Leonardo the Terrible Monster*.

Sharing the Story Lesson

- Sing the *Marching Monsters Race* song.

- Discuss the feelings listed in the song using the graphics that show the monster's faces/feelings.

- Call on kids to make up explanations for the monsters that had no description of their expressions, telling why the monsters felt the way they did during the race. (Ex. Monster One was determined because he wanted to win.)

- Read *Leonardo the Terrible Monster* aloud.

- Share positive and negative ways to deal with feelings.

- Discuss ways to resolve negative feelings safely and/or with peace of mind.

Check for Understanding

- Ask them to listen carefully as you describe situations.

- Tell them to make their faces show how they would feel if these things really happened.

- State the situations and assess the children's comprehension of feelings and facial expressions with their personal responses.

  1. Your new puppy ran away and never came back.

  2. Your dog chewed your favorite toy all to pieces.

  3. Your cousin tried to swim in a mud puddle.

  4. Your mom cooked your favorite food for dinner.

Recommended Bibliography

Fiction

Amanda Pig and the Awful, Scary Monster by Jean Van Leeuwen. Puffin, 2004.

Clara Ann Cookie by Harriet Ziefert. Houghton Mifflin, 1999.

A Dark, Dark Tale by Ruth Brown. Delmar Publishers, 1991.

Dear Big, Mean, Ugly Monster by Ruth M. Berglin. Child & Family Press, 2005.

Frank Was a Monster Who Wanted to Dance by Keith Graves. Chronicle Books, 1999.

Glad Monster, Sad Monster: A Book about Feelings by Ed Emberley. Little, Brown and Company, 1997. (Fold-out masks included.)

Go Away, Big Green Monster! by Ed Emberley. Walker & Co., 1992. (Die-cut pages.)

Go to Bed, Monster! by Natasha Wing. Harcourt, 2007.

Grumpy Cat by Britta Teckentrup. Boxer Books, 2008.

Happy Birthday, Monster! by Scott Beck. Abrams Books for Young Readers, 2007.

Hungry Monster ABC: An Alphabet Book by Susan Heyboer O'Keefe. Little, Brown and Company, 2007.

Junie B. Jones Has a Monster Under Her Bed by Barbara Park. Random House, 1997.

Leonardo the Terrible Monster by Mo Willems. Walker & Co., 2008.

The Lima Bean Monster by Dan Yaccarino. Walker & Co., 2001.

Monster Countdown by Pamela Jane. Mondo, 2001.

Monster Goes to School by Virginia Mueller. Albert Whitman, 1991.

Monster Hug! by David Ezra Stein. Putnam, 2007.

Monster Manners by Bethany Roberts. Clarion Books, 1996.

Monster Math by Grace Maccarone. Scholastic, 1995.

Monster Math by Anne Miranda. Harcourt, 2002.

Monster Math Picnic by Grace Maccarone. Scholastic, 1998.

Monster Math School Time by Grace Maccarone. Scholastic, 1997.

Monster Toddler by John Wallace. Hyperion Books for Children, 2003.

My Monster Mama Loves Me So by Laura Leuck. HarperCollins, 2002.

Mud Puddle by Robert Munsch. Annick Press, 2003.

The Sea Monster by Christopher Wormell. Transworld Publishers, 2006.

That Makes Me Mad! by Steven Kroll. SeaStar Books, 2002.

Wanda's Monster by Eileen Spinelli. Albert Whitman, 2002.

When a Monster is Born by Sean Taylor. Roaring Brook Press, 2007.

Who Is Your Favorite Monster, Mama? by Barbara Shook Hazen. Hyperion Books for Children, 2006.

Where the Wild Things Are by Maurice Sendak. Red Fox, 2000.

Nonfiction

Feelings (six-title series) from Heinemann Library, 2007.

Monster Musical Chairs by Stuart J. Murphy. HarperCollins, 2001.

Monster Motel: Poems and Paintings by Douglas Florian. Harcourt Brace, 1998.

Monster Poems compiled by John Foster. Oxford University Press, 2008.

Web Sites

Kids Health. kidshealth.org/kid/talk/kidssay/comments_scared.html. Kids talk about feeling scared.

Little Kids' Games Online. www.littlekidsgamesonline.com/halloween-party-games-for-kids.html. See instructions for *Monster Statues.*

Mind Games for Kids, Brain Games for Children, Party Games, Brainteasers, Mind … www.4to40.com/games/print.asp?gid=25. Mummy Wrap Game: Kids love to act like scary monsters, and this game gives them a chance to do just that. It's also a great icebreaker for kids who don't know each other very well.

NIEHS Kids' Pages. kids.niehs.nih.gov/lyrics/johnny.htm. Melody and lyrics for *When Johnny Comes Marching Home Again.*

Marching Monster Race

Sing to the refrain of *When Johnny Comes Marching Home Again.*

Aileen Kirkham, ©2009

Monsters march in a number line, 1, 2, 3, 4.

Monsters march in a number line, 5, 6, 7, 8.

Monsters march in a number line with 9 and 10 at the end

Let's find out who'll win the Marching Monster Race.

Monster 1 has a scary face. I wonder, why?

Monster 2 has a funny face. I wonder, why?

Monster 3 has a very sad face, no one let her win a race.

Let's count on to learn the feelings of them all.

Monster 4 looks so surprised. I wonder, why?

Monster 5 has a happy face. I wonder, why?

Monster 6 has a frowny face, he wants to win this monster race.

Let's count on to learn the feelings of them all.

Monster 7 has a thoughtful face, I wonder why?

Monster 8 has an angry face, I wonder, why?

Monster 9 has a serious face, she's wondering how to win this race.

Let's count on to learn the feelings of them all.

Monster 10 has a fearful face, I wonder, why?

Monster 10 has a fearful face, I wonder, why?

1 was first and 10 was last, all the monsters they marched past,

Now which one won the Marching Monster Race?

Motion in the Ocean: Animals Alive!

McRel Standards

Language Arts & Music

(Both listed in the Introduction on page 6.)

Grades K–4 History

- Understands the folklore and other cultural contributions from various regions of the United States and how they helped to form a national heritage

Science—Life Science

- Understands the relationships among organisms and their physical environment

Theater

- Uses acting skills

Thinking and Reasoning

- Understands and applies basic principles of logic and reasoning

Lesson Objectives

- Explore ocean creatures.
- Observe attributes of ocean creatures.
- Define the ocean as a habitat for creatures with unique adaptations.
- Manipulate puppets in an African folktale play.
- Listen for ordinal number cues to dramatize a story.
- Experience measurement terminology to comprehend meaning from text.

Introduce the Lesson

Preparation

- Make a transparency of the ocean song on page 104 for the kids to see and sing along.
- Bookmark the Web sites (see this section's bibliography for recommended sites).
- Use the shark and coral puppet patterns found on page 103.

Presentation

- Display the words of the song when you introduce the lesson.
- Demonstrate the motions for the kids to use for each verse.
- Use the coral and the shark puppet to sing the *Ocean Song* on page 104 while the kids are "swimming."
- Ask students to name the two creatures in the song that live in the ocean.
- View the pictures of sharks and coral from the National Geographic Web pages.
- Discuss whether or not a shark is helpful or harmful to other ocean creatures.
- Explain that coral eats small things, and also protects and provides for many sea creatures.

Sharing the Story Lesson

Preparation

- Select and display an assortment of fiction and nonfiction books about ocean animals, including the coral reef.

Presentation

- Picture read or read a nonfiction book about the coral reef aloud. I recommend Sylvia A. Earle's *Coral Reefs* and *Hello Fish! Visiting the Coral Reef*, or *Coral Reefs* by Gail Gibbons.

- Reiterate the importance of the coral reef to other ocean creatures.

Check for Understanding

- Use the transparency to sing the *Ocean Song* again.

- Challenge students to name ways that coral is important.

- Optional: show students the book, *Way Down in the Deep Blue Sea*.

  Give them three clues to guess what the pretend ocean/sea actually is in the little boy's house. Show them the cover of the book.

  1. It's in the room of your house where there is a sink and a toilet.

  2. It's long and deep thing. (Show size with hands.)

  3. You can sit in it.

     What is it? (bathtub)

     "Okay if you can't guess it, here's another clue."

  4. You take a bath in it.

     Read the book if time permits.

Extension Activity: Folktale Adaption of "Why the Sun and the Moon Live in the Sky"

Preparation

- Make a class set of the shark and coral puppets on page 103 and other sea creature puppets on pages 105–107 (one puppet per child). Use the paint sticks as directed in the shark and coral puppet directions to mount the other sea creature puppets. Home improvement stores often give away paint sticks if they're to be used for a non-profit group.)

- Copy the adapted folktale on pages 108–109 and place in a page protector for the play.

Presentation

- Recite this rhyme:

  I see you in the ocean, I see you in the sea.

  (Sway like in a wave holding binoculars to see the kids.)

  Let's share a folktale! Come closer to me.

  (Sweep your hands as if you are gathering the kids toward you.)

- Explain that a folktale is a very old story that storytellers made up and then told to people everywhere since there was no TV in those days of long ago.

- Share the rules of puppetry etiquette found on page 7 of the introduction.

- Name each ocean creature as you show the kids the stick puppets.

- Tell them they will each get a puppet to participate in the puppet play.

- Tell them you will read the story script out loud. At your verbal (name of animal) and physical cue (pointing your finger), they will move toward you into the "imaginary" house of Sun and Moon.

- Divide the students into five groups: coral, seahorses, starfish, octopuses, and sharks.

- Direct them to watch you and listen carefully to the words of the play to know when it's their puppet pal's turn to swim into the house.

- Pass out the puppets and perform the play.

Check for Understanding

- Show them where they need to bring their puppets to live at school (storage containers).

- Collect the puppets by naming the ocean creatures' attributes:
  1. I have huge teeth to grab and chomp things. (Shark)
  2. I have five "arms" that move slowly in the sea instead of twinkling in the sky. (Starfish)
  3. I swim in the sea instead of having a rodeo cowboy on my back. (Seahorse)
  4. I am as hard as a rock and I live on the ocean floor. (Coral)
  5. I look like a balloon with eight legs. (Octopus)

Recommended Bibliography

Fiction

Over in the Ocean: In a Coral Reef by Marianne Collins Berkes. Dawn Publications, 2004.

Somewhere in the Ocean by Jennifer Ward and T. J. Marsh. Rising Moon, 2000.

Under the Sea by Liza Baker. HarperFestival, 2003.

Way Down Deep in the Deep Blue Sea by Jan Peck. Simon & Shuster, 2004.

Nonfiction

All About Sharks by Jim Arnosky. Scholastic, 2003.

Clown Fish and Other Coral Reef Life by Sally Morgan. QEB Publishing, 2008.

Coral Reef Animals by Francine Galko. Heinemann Library, 2003.

Coral Reefs by Sylvia A. Earle. National Geographic, 2003.

Coral Reefs by Gail Gibbons. Holiday House, 2007.

Hello Fish! Visiting the Coral Reef by Sylvia A. Earle. National Geographic, 2001.

Life in an Ocean by Carol K. Lindeen. Captstone Press, 2004.

Pebble Plus: Under the Sea (series) by Capstone Press, 2005–2008.

Sharks: Hunters of the Deep (series) by PowerKids Press, 2007.

Sharks: Biggest! Littlest! by Sandra Markle. Boyds Mills Press, 2008.

Sharks! Strange and Wonderful by Laurence Pringle. Boyds Mills Press, 2008.

Surprising Sharks by Nicola Davies. Candlewick Press, 2008.

Why the Sun and the Moon Live in the Sky: An African Folktale by Elphinstone Dayrell. Scholastic, 1991.

Professional Books

Tide Pools and Coral Reefs by Jeanne King. Teacher Created Materials, 1993.

Web Sites

Kid Cyber: What is Coral? www.kidcyber.com.au/topics/coral.htm. Explanation via text and images.

Enchanted Learning: What is a Shark? www.enchantedlearning.com/subjects/sharks/allabout. Detailed explanation and information, including charts and diagrams.

National Geographic: Great White Shark. animals.nationalgeographic.com/animals/fish/great-white-shark.html. Profile, features, fast facts, images, and more.

Shark and Coral Puppet Patterns

Copy each pattern onto cardstock or glue them onto file folders.
Color*, cut out, and laminate them for durability.
Then, glue, tack, or staple each to the tops of a paint sticks to make stick puppets.

*Eliminate coloring step by copying the patterns directly onto appropariately colored cardstock.

Ocean Song

Sing to the tune of *She'll Be Comin' Round the Mountain*. Shout the bolded words.
Aileen Kirkham, ©2008.

Oh! We're swimming in the ocean having fun, **having fun.**

Oh! We're swimming in the ocean having fun, **having fun.**

Oh! We're swimming in the ocean,
Oh! We're swimming in the ocean,
Oh! We're swimming in the ocean having fun, **having fun.**

Oh! That shark is looking hungry, time to eat, **swim faster!**

Oh! That shark is looking hungry, time to eat, **swim faster!**

Oh! That shark is looking hungry,
Oh! That shark is looking hungry,
Oh! That shark is looking hungry, time to eat. **swim faster!**

Oh! Let's hide in the coral, out of sight, **out of sight.**

Oh! Let's hide in the coral, out of sight, **out of sight.**

Oh! Let's hide in the coral,
Oh! Let's hide in the coral,
Oh! Let's hide in the coral, out of sight, **out of sight.**

Sea Creature Puppet Pattern: Octopus

Copy each pattern onto cardstock or glue them onto file folders.
Color*, cut out, and laminate them for durability.
Then, glue, tack, or staple each to the tops of a paint sticks to make stick puppets.

*Eliminate coloring step by copying the patterns directly onto appropriately-colored cardstock.

Sea Creature Puppet Pattern: Starfish

Copy each pattern onto cardstock or glue them onto file folders.
Color*, cut out, and laminate them for durability.
Then, glue, tack, or staple each to the tops of a paint sticks to make stick puppets.

*Eliminate coloring step by copying the patterns directly onto appropriately-colored cardstock.

Sea Creature Puppet Pattern: Seahorse

Copy each pattern onto cardstock or glue them onto file folders.
Color*, cut out, and laminate them for durability.
Then, glue, tack, or staple each to the tops of a paint sticks to make stick puppets.

*Eliminate coloring step by copying the patterns directly onto appropriately-colored cardstock.

Why the Sun and the Moon Live in the Sky

A folktale adapted by Aileen Kirkham, ©2008.

Sun and Moon lived alone in their house in Africa. One day Sun said, "Moon, my beautiful wife, it is very lonely here, I wish my friend Water would come for a visit." Moon replied, "Send a message with Pelican the Postman to your friend."

Sun agreed, "That's a wonderful idea." He wrote:

Dear Water,

You are invited to come to visit Moon and me as soon as possible.

Your friend,
Sun

Pelican picked up the letter and brought back Water's answer the next day.

Dear Sun,

I cannot come to visit you. Your house is too small for me and all of my family.

Your friend,
Water

Sun was very sad when he got the message. "Moon, Water said our house is too small. What should we do?"

Moon smiled wisely and said, "We'll build it bigger, so big that Water and all of his family will fit just fine."

So Sun and Moon worked day and night. They worked very hard and built the house taller and wider. When they were finished, Sun wrote another message and gave it to Pelican the Postman.

Dear Water,

We built our house much taller and much wider. You and your family can fit inside now. Come and visit as soon as you can.

Your Friend,
Sun

Pelican the Postman flew back bright and early the next day with Water's response.

Dear Sun,

My family and I would love to visit now. See you soon.

Your friend,
Water

Sun and Moon waited anxiously on the front porch and shined brightly when they saw Water flowing up the road. They opened the door and called out, "Come in! Come in!"

Water bubbled happily through the door and behind him came all his relatives:

First came coral who covered all the floor. Sun and Moon moved up off the floor to sit on the window sills.

Second came the seahorses who rode in on waves. Sun and Moon moved up higher to sit on the kitchen cabinets.

Third came the starfish from smallest to largest. Sun and Moon moved up higher to the ceiling.

Fourth came the small and giant octopuses. Sun and Moon move up higher to sit on top of the roof.

Fifth came the sharks. Sun and Moon moved up higher until they were sitting in the sky.

Sun and Moon said, "Oh! My! When we're up this high, we can see our friends all over the world. This is the perfect place for us!"

So that is why even today, Sun and Moon live in the sky. The End.

Nighty-Night Delights & Family Reading Nights

McRel Standards

Language Arts & Music

(Both listed in the Introduction on page 6.)

Behavioral Studies

- Understands that interactions among learning, inheritance, and physical development affect human behavior

Health

- Knows how to maintain and promote personal health

Mathematics

- Understands and applies basic and advanced properties of the concepts of numbers

Lesson Objectives

- Sing a song to make a one-to-one correspondence between reading and bedtime.
- Identify the need to select books to take home and read.
- Establish a bedtime routine that includes books.
- Participate in a pajama party to share good books.

Introduce the Lesson: Nighty-Night, Book Delights

Preparation

- Make a child-size bed from a box, cover it with a blanket, add a pillow, some bedtime books from the lesson's bibliography, and a teddy bear. (Optional: Use an air mattress to make the bed.)
- Make a transparency of the song from page 114, *Nighty-Night Delights* for students to see and sing along.
- Optional: Make a bear puppet from the pattern on page 115 so the bear can sing the song.
- Optional: Librarian/teacher wears pajamas to do the lesson.

Presentation

- Point to the bed display and ask the kids what they need to go to bed at night. Accept all responses, but if they forget to say a book, then ask them to guess something very important to do each night in bed. Take three guesses to try to get the answer of "a book." Give clues as needed: it has pages, it has words and pictures, you check them out at the library, etc.
- Display the *Nighty-Night Delights* song.
- Direct the children to echo sing the song *Nighty-Night Delights* on page 114. Tell them you (or the bear puppet) will sing first, then they will repeat it.

  *Explain the meaning of "picture reading" as making up the story to match the pictures. Tell them they can picture read when an older reader can't read to them.

Sharing the Story Lesson

Preparation

- Select and display a variety of bedtime books from the lesson's bibliography.

Presentation

- Direct the kids to play "Nighty-Night Copy-cat." (They copy each action you model.)

    1. Yawn and stretch loudly.

    2. Take a splashy, sudsy bath. (Good hygiene reminder.)

    3. Brush your teeth. (Good hygiene reminder.)

    4. Climb into bed without a book, then snap your finger beside your face like you just remembered something and say, "OOPS! I forgot to do something VERY important before I went to sleep."

    Point to the Nighty-Night Book Delights display and tell the kids that all of these are wonderful books to picture read alone or have read aloud by their family members and friends.

- Read one book aloud from the display that relates to the theme of the song such as *I Am Not Sleepy and I Will Not Go to Bed*; *Llama, Llama Red Pajama*; *Looking for Sleepy*; or *Otto Goes to Bed*.

- Emphasize the importance of a good night's sleep which is why parents make kids have a bedtime. (Share this in a humorous way such as they don't want you to fall asleep in your cereal the next morning, or go to sleep on the bus and forget to go to school, or be too sleepy to play, etc. Dramatize scenarios.)

Check for Understanding

- Use the transparency to sing the song again to reiterate the importance of reading books at bedtime.

- Challenge students to demonstrate a nighty-night routine with your cues:

    1. Yawn.
    (Let them make the sound.)

    2. Bathe.
    (Dramatize getting into the shower.)

    3. Brush.
    (Show your teeth.)

    4. Climb into bed, snap your fingers, and open your mouth to say, "OOPS! I forgot to do something important. What can it be?"

- Encourage students to select books from the display to take home for bedtime reading.

Extension Activity: Nighty-Night Delights Pajama Party

- View ideas for how to set up a Family Reading Night at www.librarysparks.com. Click on the Web Resources link on the homepage, then scroll down to the bottom and click on the February 2005 link. Click on *New! Keep'em Reading: Family Literacy Night*. This is an article I wrote after doing literacy nights for 10+ years.

- Work with your principal to set aside a Nighty-Night Delights Pajama Party for all grade levels.

- Advertise the event with your staff and/or families as a beneficial literary event.

- Sing or say the *Nighty-Night Delights* song during announcements each day to remind students of the upcoming event.

- Make giveaway bookmarks with recommended read-alouds for each grade level including the titles read during the event.

- Encourage students to bring their favorite stuffed animal friend to the event, too.

    (Pillows might also be brought as long as the students are reminded NOT to share them due to the possibility of lice.)

- Scheduling Options:

    1. Daytime event with upper and lower grades paired together for reading together—work with teaching staff to make a schedule for the day.

2. Evening event with parents/families—if held as a night-time reading event, you may wish to have a time set aside (10–15 min.) for parent/child story time to read together and schedule the services of a professional storyteller to follow. (Optional: Cookies and milk could be served at the end of the evening, too.) Pass out bookmarks with recommended read alouds for all grade levels.

Recommended Bibliography

Fiction

All on a Sleepy Night by Shutta Crum. Stoddart Kids, 2001.

Are You Ready for Bed? by Jane Johnson. Tiger Tales, 2002.

Arctic Dreams by Carole Gerber. Charlesbridge, 2005.

Bear Dreams by Elisha Cooper. Greenwillow Books, 2006.

Bed Hogs by Kelly S. DiPucchio. Hyperion Books for Children, 2004.

Ben Over Night by Sarah Ellis. Fitzhenry & Whiteside, 2005.

The Boy Who Wouldn't Go to Bed by Helen Cooper. Penguin Putnam, 2000.

Bubba and Beau Go Night-Night by Kathi Appelt. Harcourt, 2003.

Clara Ann Cookie, Go to Bed! by Harriet Ziefert. Houghton Mifflin, 2000.

Cornelius P. Mud, Are You Ready for Bed? by Barney Saltzberg. Candlewick Press, 2007.

Froggy Goes to Bed by Jonathan London. Red Fox, 2001.

Go to Bed, Monster! by Natasha Wing. Harcourt, 2007.

Goodnight Baxter by Nicola Edwards. Running Kids Press, 2004.

Goodnight Lulu by Paulette Bogan. Bloomsbury Publishing, 2005.

Goodnight, Me by Andrew Daddo. Bloomsbury Children's Books, 2007.

Goodnight Me, Goodnight You by Tony Mitton. Orchard Books, 2003.

Goodnight Moon by Margaret Wise Brown. HarperTrophy, 2005.

Goodnight, Sweet Pig by Linda Bailey. Kids Can Press, 2007.

The Goodnight Train by June Sobel. Harcourt, 2006.

I Am Not Sleepy and I Will Not Go to Bed by Lauren Child. Candlewick Press, 2005.

Junie B. Jones Has a Monster Under Her Bed by Barbara Park. Random House, 1997.

Llama, Llama Red Pajama by Anna Dewdney. Viking, 2005.

Looking for Sleepy by Maribeth Boelts. Albert Whitman, 2004.

Mermaid Dreams by Mark Sperring. Scholastic, 2006.

Noah's Bed by Lis Coplestone. Frances Lincoln, 2006.

The Noisy Way to Bed by Ian Whybrow. Arthur A. Levine, 2004.

Otto Goes to Bed by Todd Parr. Little, Brown and Company, 2003.

The Prince Won't Go to Bed! by Dayle Ann Dodds. Farrar, Straus and Giroux, 2007.

Rabbit's Pajama Party by Stuart J. Murphy. HarperCollins, 1999.

Sleepy Boy by Polly Kanevsky. Atheneum, 2006.

Sleepy Little Owl by Howard Goldsmith. Learning Triangle Press, 1997.

Sleepy Places by Judy Hindley. Candlewick Press, 2006.

Snuggle Up, Sleepy Ones by Claire Freedman. Good Books, 2007.

So Sleepy Story by Uri Shulevitz. Farrar, Straus and Giroux, 2006.

Song of Night: It's Time to Go to Bed by Katherine Riley Nakamura. Blue Sky Press, 2002.

The Stuffed Animals Get Ready for Bed by Alison Inches. Harcourt, 2006.

Sweet Dreams: How Animals Sleep by Kimiko Kajikawa. Harcourt, 1999.

Time for Bed by Mem Fox. Harcourt Brace, 1997.

Web Sites

Bedtime Stories.
www.monroe.lib.in.us/childrens/bedbib.html.
A list of recommended bedtime stories and rhymes for young children.

LibrarySparks.
www.librarysparks.com. The Web site for the magazine for school and public children's librarians.

Texas Library Association.
www.txla.org.
Click on the "READING LISTS" link, then click on "2X2 Age two through second grade." Each year a new list of 20 books is selected by a committee of Texas public and school librarians from highly recommended books published in that calendar year. There are many, many books from these lists that can be found in libraries across the U.S. All are recommended as read alouds for young children in grades PK–2.

Nighty-Night Delights

Sung to the tune of *Mary Had a Little Lamb.*

**Don't forget to read at night,
read at night, read at night.**

**Don't forget to read at night
so pick some nighty-night delights.**

**Who will read these books to you,
these books to you, these books to you?**

**Who will read these books to you,
Your parents, friends, and you can, too.**

Bear Puppet Pattern

Copy the pattern onto cardstock/tagboard. Then color, cut out, and glue it to the top of a paint stick to create a stick puppet. For durability, laminate before gluing.

Penguin Perspectives: Olympic Movements

McRel Standards

Language Arts & Music

(Both listed in the Introduction on page 6.)

Mathematics

- Understands and applies basic and advanced properties of the concepts of numbers.

Science—Life Sciences

- Understands the relationships among organisms and their physical environment

Lesson Objectives

- Compute the total number of penguins.
- View the physical attributes of penguins.
- Explore the habitats of penguins.
- Define penguins' role in the food chain as predator and prey.
- Dramatize the movement of penguins.

Introduce the Lesson

Preparation

- Optional: make the penguin puppet on page 119 to sing the song to introduce the lesson.
- Make a transparency from page 120 of the *Penguin Pals* song for students to see and sing along. While singing, show the two-page spread of Gail Gibbon's book, *Penguins*. Point to the different kinds of penguins one by one as you sing the song.
- Bookmark the Web site www.kidzone.ws/animals/penguins/index.htm.

- Use sticky notes to place the name and average height of different types of penguins on a yardstick to compare with a child from the class.

  1. Emperor Penguins and King Penguins at four feet (you will need a ruler to add to the top of the yardstick).

  2. Adelie Penguins, Chinstrap Penguins, Gentoo Penguins, and Macaroni Penguins 27+ inches.

  3. Rockhopper Penguins at 21½ inches.

  4. Fairy Penguins at 16–17 inches.

Presentation

- Display the transparency of the *Penguin Pals* song on page 120.
- Call on a child to come and stand next to the yardstick with the sticky notes of penguins' heights to compare his/her height with different types of penguins. Compare it with something as tall as what is on the child's body: tall as head, nose, elbow, etc.
- Ask how many penguins there are in the picture with 10 as the last number of the song, and then count on to 11 and 12.
- Use illustrations from Gail Gibbons' book, *Penguins*, to discuss some of the different kinds. Note their distinguishing features and the fact that some have names that identify the way they look like in the book (an Adelie has a heart-shaped white front). Or, click on the link, Penguin Photos at www.kidzone.ws/animals/penguins/index.htm.

Sharing the Story Lesson

Preparation

- Select and display a variety of fiction and nonfiction penguin books.

- Make a transparency of the song *Penguin Perspectives* on page 121 for children to see and sing along.

- Optional: Obtain a VCR or DVD player to view *Antarctic Antics*.

Presentation

- Display the transparency and sing the *Penguin Perspectives* song from page 121.

- Read aloud or watch *Antarctic Antics*, and select specific poems that reinforce habitat, food chain, and movement.

   (The DVD/video, *Antarctic Antics*, is excellent and can be stopped for discussion to reinforce concepts in lesson: habitat, food chain, and movement. As necessary, skip over the harder to understand poems to experience penguin life in a kid-friendly cartoon format.)

- Discuss

   1. Type of Penguin (Emperor: largest)

   2. Type of Habitat

   3. Food Chain (food preferences and predators)

   4. Movement (Note unique attributes of tobogganing and inability to fly.)

- Review habitat, food chain, and movements by singing, modeling, and dramatizing.

Check for Understanding

- Use the transparency to sing the song again to reiterate the scientific attributes of penguins.

- Challenge students to name at least three kinds of penguins from the lesson.

- Encourage students to check out penguin books to picture read and do read alouds with their families and friends.

Extension Activity: Penguin Olympics!

Preparation

- Locate *Tacky and the Winter Games*.

- Mark off start and stop lines for the class' reenactment of the games.

Sharing the Story Lesson

- Tell the students to look and listen to how the games are played in *Tacky and the Winter Games*.

- Read *Tacky and the Winter Games* aloud.

- Ask students to list which games they could play in the classroom to reenact the story.

- Divide the class into teams.

- Model the movement each team does for each Olympics-style relay.

- Show the teams the pre-marked start and stop lines.

- Specify the signal that will start each relay.

- Monitor movements for safe play.

Check for Understanding

- Ask students to name the types of penguin movements used in the class' Penguin Olympics.

- Challenge students to think of other types of penguin games/movements that the author could have included in *Tacky and the Winter Games*.

Recommended Bibliography

Fiction

I Am Pangoo the Penguin by Satomi Ichikawa. Philomel Books, 2006.

The Little Penguin by Audrey Wood. Dutton Children's Books, 2002.

My Penguin Osbert by Elizabeth Cody Kimmel. Candlewick Press, 2004.

Penguin by Polly Dunbar. Candlewick Press, 2007.

Penguin and Little Blue by Megan McDonald. Atheneum, 2003.

A Penguin Pup for Pinkerton by Steven Kellogg. Puffin, 2003.

Tacky and the Winter Games by Helen Lester. Houghton Mifflin, 2007. (One title in a series of Tacky books.)

Tina and the Penguin by Heather Dyer. Kids Can Press, 2002.

Nonfiction

Antarctic Antics: A Book of Penguin Poems by Judy Sierra. Harcourt, 2003.

Baby Penguin by Aubrey Lang. Fitzhenry and Whiteside, 2002.

The Life Cycle of a Penguin by Lisa Trumbauer. Pebble Books, 2004.

Macaroni Penguin by Edana Eckart. Children's Press, 2005.

Penguin Chick by Betty Tatham. HarperCollins, 2002.

A Penguin Chick Grows Up by Joan Hewett. Carolrhoda Books, 2004.

A Penguin's World by Caroline Arnold. Picture Window Books, 2006.

Penguins! by Gail Gibbons. Holiday House, 2000.

Penguins ABC by Kevin Schafer. NorthWood Press, 2004.

Penguins 1, 2, 3 by Kevin Schafer. NorthWood Press, 2002.

Multimedia

Antarctic Antics: A Book of Penguins, Scholastic, 2007. (Purchase at www.libraryvideo.com.)

Web Sites

About Antarctica. www.antarcticconnection.com/antarctic/wild-life/penguins/fairy.shtml. Natural history information about fairy penguins.

KidZone. www.kidzone.ws/animals/penguins/index.htm. Penguin activities, facts, and photos.

Library Video. www.library video.com. National distributor of educational videos, DVDs, and audiobooks to schools and public libraries.

Penguins. lrs.ed.uiuc.edu/students/downey/project/penguins.html. Natural history information and photos of a variety of penguin species.

Emperor Penguin Puppet Pattern

Copy the pattern onto cardstock/tagboard. Then color, cut out, and glue it to the top of a paint stick to create a stick puppet. For durability, laminate before gluing.

Penguin Pals

(Sing to the tune of *10 Little Indians*)

Aileen Kirkham, ©2007

Emperor • Macaroni • King • Chinstrap • Little Blue/Fairy • Rockhopper

1 little, 2 little, 3 little penguin pals,
4 little, 5 little, 6 little penguin pals
7 little, 8 little, 9 little penguin pals,
10 penguin pals, plus 2.

Not all of them look just alike,
Not all of them look just alike
Not all of them look just alike,
Since there are different kinds.

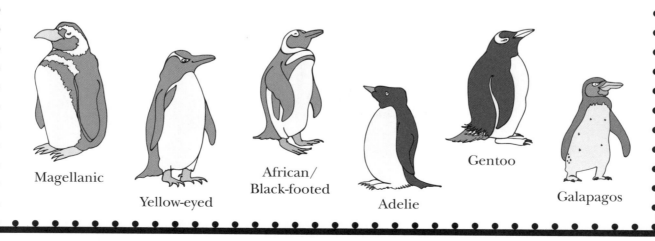

Magellanic • Yellow-eyed • African/Black-footed • Adelie • Gentoo • Galapagos

Penguin Perspectives

Sing to the tune of *London Bridge is Falling Down* and demonstrate movements.

Aileen Kirkham, ©2007

If you were a penguin you'd waddle like this,
waddle like this,
waddle like this,
If you were a penguin you'd waddle like this
upon the icy shore.

If you were a penguin, you'd swim like this,
swim like this,
swim like this.
If you were a penguin, you'd swim like this
in the ocean deep.

If you were a penguin, you'd eat like this,
eat like this,
eat like this.
If you were a penguin, you'd eat like this
to swallow down your fish.

A penguin can be small or tall,
small or tall, small or tall,
A penguin can be small or tall
since there are different kinds.

Pets to Ponder:
Shapes

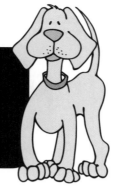

McRel Standards

Language Arts & Music

(Both listed in the Introduction on page 6.)

Mathematics

- Understands and applies basic and advanced properties of the concepts of geometry

Lesson Objectives

- Identify and name basic shapes: circles, triangles, ovals, rectangles, and squares.

- Use basic shapes to create a puppet and/or solve a puzzle.

Introduce the Lesson:
Kittens and Puppies song

Preparation

- Make an example of the envelope puppet pets with glued-on shapes found on pages 125–126. Make one dog and one cat.

- Make a transparency of the *Kittens and Puppies* song on page 127 for students to see and sing along.

Presentation

- Display the *Kittens and Puppies* song and ask the students if they know the names of the shapes at the top. Solicit three guesses for each, and then give correct name. Further clarification may be given for an oval by saying it is a stretched circle. The same clarification applies to a rectangle, since it looks like a stretched square.

- Explain that shapes can be combined to create pictures.

- Direct the children to echo sing the song *Kitten and Puppies* from page 127 with the puppy and kitten puppet pals singing first, and then the kids will repeat the line.

- Challenge students to join you as you count the number of each kind of shape in both the kitten and puppy pets.

Sharing the Story Lesson

Preparation

- Select and display a variety of shape and pet books.

- Select one of the Lois Ehlert books to read aloud: *Feathers for Lunch* (cat) or *Wag a Tail* (dog).

- Select a simplistic nonfiction information book about shapes.

Presentation

- Read the Ehlert book aloud and remind kids to notice all the different shapes that were put together to make the cat or dog on each page.

- Picture read the simplistic nonfiction information book about shapes to reinforce the names of the basic shapes.

Check for Understanding

- Use the transparency to sing the song again to reinforce the names of the basic shapes.

- Challenge students to come forward one at a time and name one shape seen on each page of the Lois Ehlert book. You may wish to give them the name of the shape to find as an assessment of their knowledge.

OR

- Play the *Fun With Shapes* game at www.Kid-spsych.org/gooochy2.html.

  After each piece of puzzle is placed, ask them what shape the puzzle piece was.

  (Please note that some of the puzzle pieces aren't basic shapes; let them know if it is an irregular shape.)

Extension Activity: Make & Take a Pet Puppet

Preparation

- Buy a tub of fun foam shapes (Hobby Lobby, Michael's, Wal-Mart, etc.) or precut shapes for animal features from construction paper. A die-cut machine would work for this, too.

- Get 4 ⅛" x 9 ½" white business letter envelopes, one or two per child with a few extras for mistakes.

- Get craft glue.

- Use the dog and cat envelope puppet examples according to the pattern on pages 125–126 that you made for the introduction.

Share the Story Lesson

- Use the transparency and envelope pet puppets to sing the *Kittens and Puppies* song.

- Read aloud *The Best Pet Yet!, Kitty Up!,* or *The Way I Love You!*

- Explain that each child will get to make a dog or cat/both kinds of envelope puppet.

- Show them how to lick and stick their precut envelope flaps.

- Let them choose which one they would like for a puppet pet.

- Show them how to make their puppets.

Check for Understanding

- Ask each child to share the name of one they used for their pet's eye, nose, whiskers (rectangles), mouth, or ears.

- Direct the kids to use their pet puppets to sing the songs again.

- Keep puppet pets at school to use during the shapes unit. Then allow students to take their puppets home. If paper is available, give them a copy of the song to share with their families, too.

Recommended Bibliography

Fiction

The Best Pet of All by David LaRochelle. Dutton Children's Books, 2004.

Duck at the Door by Jackie Urbanovic. HarperCollins, 2007.

Feathers for Lunch by Lois Ehlert. Harcourt, 1996.

Kitty Up! by Elizabeth Wojtusik. Dial, 2008.

Mouse Shapes by Ellen Stoll Walsh. Harcourt, 2007.

Round Is a Mooncake: a Book of Shapes by Roseanne Thong. Chronicle Books, 2000.

Three Pigs, One Wolf, and Seven Magic Shapes by Grace Maccarone. Scholastic, 1997.*

Wag a Tail by Lois Ehlert. Harcourt, 2007.

The Way I Love You by David Bedford. Simon & Schuster, 2005.

Nonfiction

Caring for Your Pets: A Book about Veterinarians by Ann Owen. Picture Window Books, 2004.

Combining Shapes by Jennifer Boothroyd. LernerClassroom, 2007.*

Dogku by Andrew Clements. Simon & Schuster, 2007.

Drawing and Learning about Cats: Using Shapes and Lines by Amy Bailey Muehlenhardt. Picture Window Books, 2004.*

Drawing and Learning about Dogs: Using Shapes and Lines by Amy Bailey Muehlenhardt. Picture Window Books, 2004.*

Eye Spy Shapes by Debbie MacKinnon. Frances Lincoln, 2001.

First Facts: Positively Pets (series) from Capstone Press, 2007.

Fun Crafts with Shapes by Jordina Ros. Enslow Elementary, 2006.

Icky Bug Shapes by Jerry Palotta. Scholastic, 2004.

Let's Read About Pets (series) from Weekly Reader Early Learning, 2004.

Pets ABC: An Alphabet Book by Michael Dahl. Capstone Press, 2005.

Pets! Pets! Pets! by Kathy Henderson. Frances Lincoln, 2004.

Pointy, Long, or Round: A Book about Animal Shapes by Patricia M. Stockland. Picture Window Books, 2005.*

* Books that challenge advanced learners.

Professional Books

101 Colors and Shapes Activities: Ages 3-6 by Susan Hodges. McGraw-Hill, 2004.

Shapes: Preschool/Kindergarten by Education Center/Mailbox Books, 2000.

Shapes & Sizes by Teacher Created Materials, 2002.

Storytelling with Shapes & Numbers by Valerie Marsh. Alleyside Press, 1999.

Web Sites

Games for Children Ages 1 to 5. www.kidspsych.org/gooochy2.html. Click on *Fun With Shapes* to form a mystery picture.

Kitty & Puppy Pet Puppet Instructions

Preparation

1. Fold unsealed business envelope (no larger than 4 ⅛ x 9 ½") widthwise in half to make a crease.

2. Unfold the envelope and open the envelope flap. Cut the flap in half along the crease that you just made in it.

3. Now cut along the crease on the **back of the envelope** *only.* (This will require inserting one blade of the scissors inside the envelope.)

4. Prepare enough envelopes for each child to have one (or two, if they will be making both pets)

5. Photocopy the kitty and puppy pet puppet shapes on page 126, making enough for each student to have one.

Making the Puppet

1. Instruct students to seal their envelopes by licking the envelope flaps and adhering them to the envelope.

2. Instruct students to turn the sealed envelope over so that the front is face up (the sealed flap should be facing down). They should be looking at a blank envelope with a crease in the middle.

3. Have students color in the bottom half of the envelope whichever color they'd like their pet to be.

4. Have students color in their kitty and/or puppy face shapes, and then cut them out.

5. Explain that they can create a kitty or puppy puppet by decorating the **bottom half of the envelope below the crease that they just colored in,** using glue and kitty/puppy shapes. Demonstrate if necessary. When they are finished gluing the face pieces on, they can re-fold the envelope and glue the tongue shape to the bottom half of the "mouth."

6. When all the glue is dry, demonstrate how to slide your hand into the puppet to make it move and meow/bark!

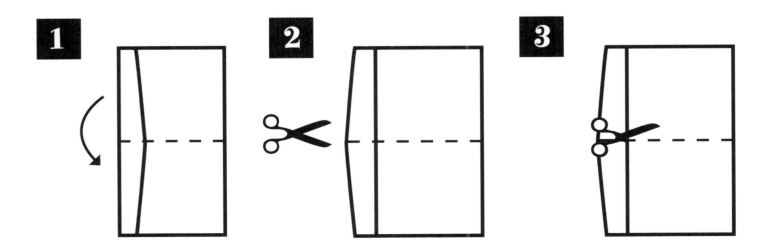

Kitty & Puppy Pet Puppet Shapes

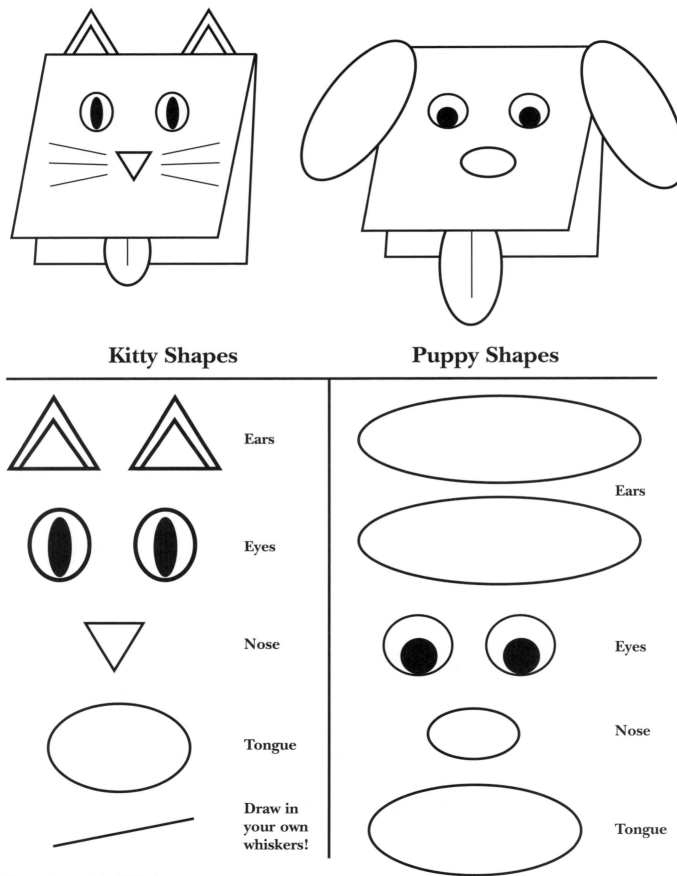

Kitty Shapes

Ears

Eyes

Nose

Tongue

Draw in your own whiskers!

Puppy Shapes

Ears

Eyes

Nose

Tongue

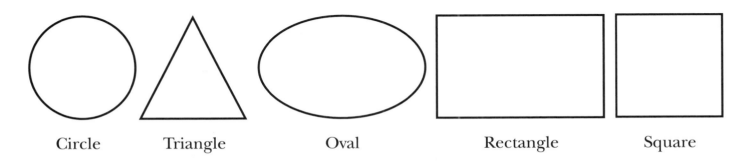

Circle   Triangle   Oval   Rectangle   Square

Kittens and Puppies

(Sung to the tune of *Frère Jacques*)

Aileen Kirkham, ©2009

Kittens and puppies, kittens and puppies,

Made from shapes, Made from shapes.

Triangles and ovals,

Circles and rectangles

Square shapes, too.

Square shapes, too.

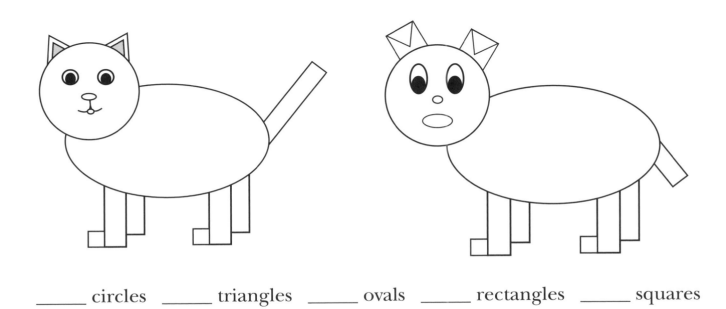

_____ circles   _____ triangles   _____ ovals   _____ rectangles   _____ squares

Ranch Wranglers:
Rodeo Rationale

McRel Standards

Language Arts & Music

(Both listed in the Introduction on page 6.)

Agricultural Education: Agriculture in History & Society

- Understands trends, issues, and events that have influenced agricultural practices throughout history

Agricultural Education: Animal/Plant/ Resource Handling

- Understands essential elements of plant and animal care

Behavioral Studies

- Understands that group and cultural influences contribute to human development, identity, and behavior

- Understands various meanings of social group, general implications of group membership, and different ways that groups function

- Understands that interactions among learning, inheritance, and physical development affect human behavior

- Understands conflict, cooperation, and interdependence among individuals, groups, and institutions

Geography: Human Systems

- Understands the patterns of human settlement and their causes

Geography: Uses of Geography

- Understands how geography is used to interpret the past

Grades K–4 History: Living and Working Together in Families and Communities, Now and Long Ago

- Understands the history of the local community and how communities in North America varied long ago

Grades K–4 History: The History of Students' Own State or Region

- Understands the people, events, problems, and ideas that were significant in creating the history of their state

Grades K–4 History: The History of Peoples of Many Cultures Around the World

- Understands the folklore and other cultural contributions from various regions of the United States and how they helped to form a national heritage.

Life Work

- Studies or pursues specific job interests

Theater

- Uses acting skills

Lesson Objectives

- Describe the role of cowboys and cowgirls on a ranch.

- Define the meaning of livestock.

- View and discuss the purpose of the cowboy/girl "uniform."

- Listen for cues as a puppeteer in a puppet show.

- Participate in age-appropriate rodeo events.

- Experience cowboy/cowgirl storytelling culture around a campfire.

Introduce the Lesson:
I'm a little Cowboy/Girl song

Preparation

- Make a transparency from page 136 of the song, *I'm a Little Cowboy/Girl*, for students to see and sing along.

- Get a cowboy hat, bandana, boots. Optional: spurs.*

Presentation

- Display a cowboy hat and ask students who would wear this and why.

- View and discuss the purpose of clothing and footwear worn by the cowboy.

  (The book, *Cowboy Small*, has an excellent illustration inside the cover with all these things.)

  *Make a transparency of the illustration to do this lesson if you can't borrow the genuine items.

  1. Hat – water the horse and weatherproof head from sun and rain.

  2. Bandana – covering for face when it's dusty, washcloth to clean self, and a neck warmer in cold weather

  3. Jeans – tough material so legs don't get chapped by weather and scratched by brush.

  4. Boots – heels hold feet in saddle, high tops protect legs.

  5. (Optional) Spurs – used to guide the horse.

- Demonstrate and sing the song *I'm a Little Cowboy/Girl* on page 136. Make sure to define and discuss what it means to wrestle a steer, then repeat song.

Sharing the Story Lesson

Preparation

- Borrow or make a class/group set of ranch stick puppets: pigs, chickens, horses and cows on pages 132–135 to introduce the lesson.

- Select and display a variety of cowboy, cowgirl, rodeo, horse, cow, pigs, and chicken books.

- Make a transparency or poster from *The Ranch Song* words on page 137 for students to see and sing along.

Presentation

- Read a book aloudthat depicts ranch life for a cowboy/girl such as:

  - *Cowboy* by Heather Miller

  - *Cowboy Small** by Lois Lensky

  - *I Wish I Were a Cowboy* by Ivan Bulloch

  *Old favorite, now colorized with main character being PreK/K-sized child.

- Display the *The Ranch Song* transparency from page 137. Define and discuss the term "livestock" (animals on the ranch). Then ask the students to name the people and animals on the ranch. Give clues as needed to fill in the names under each graphic.

- Direct the children to echo sing the song. Tell them the cowboy/girl will sing first, and then they will repeat that line. (Review puppet etiquette rules for students from page 7 of Introduction.)

- Teach students how the song will be performed by demonstrating that they're to raise their puppet pal high in the air each time their person or animal is named, and bring it back down beside them when that line of the song is over.

- Pass out puppets and sing the song twice to reinforce the names of people that work on a ranch and the different types of livestock.

- Call on students to be the Ranch Wranglers and round up the puppet pals to put them in a safe place.

Check for Understanding

- Call on students to name the four groups of animals that live on a ranch.

- Challenge them to name other livestock. Give sound clues as needed: sheep, turkeys, ducks, cats, dogs, etc.

- Review the need for a cowboy/girl to wear a hat.

- Encourage students to check out western heritage books: cowboys, cowgirls, ranches, rodeos, etc.

Extension Activity:
Ranch Wranglers Rodeo

Preparation

- Contact adult helpers to assist with the rodeo: parents, administrators, teachers, etc.

- Make cardboard horseshoes, borrow real horseshoes, or borrow one shoe from each child and pretend they are horseshoes.

- Locate four tubs or short wastebaskets for horseshoe targets.

- Locate a short, thin rope and a chair.

- Collect an assortment of stuffed animals (about 10) to be the livestock.

- Locate two clothesbaskets (hampers).

- Borrow a child's wagon.

- Request donations of individual snack packs (could substitute plastic food or pictures of food).

- Get some sticks and orange bulletin board paper to make a fake fire.

- Set up three or four rodeo events for the children to have a rodeo day:

  1. Horseshoes: supply a container for kids to throw them into instead of trying to "ring" a stake. If using real horseshoes, be sure to space the two areas far apart for safety purposes. The goal is to get the horseshoe in the tub.

  2. Roping Strays: get a rope and a chair. Place a stuffed animal on the chair. The goal is to touch the animal with the rope.

  3. Penning the Livestock: get two clothes baskets and a variety of stuffed animals (ranch-related, if possible: pigs, cows, horses, chickens, etc.). Divide the animals in half. Then scatter them in two areas. Participants must take their basket, "pen" the animals in their basket, run back and give the basket to the next person in line. That child takes the basket out to the pasture and releases the animals so they can "graze" (scatters them again). That person must take the empty basket back to the next person in line who must pen the animals again. The goal is to see which team can pen the fastest.

  4. Race to the Chuck Wagon: get a child's wagon and fill it with individual snack packs. Students are to race to the wagon, pick up one item, and go back to tag the next person in line. The goal is to see which team does it the fastest.

- Optional: send home a parent note asking them to dress their child as a cowboy or cowgirl: jeans, button front shirts, bandanas, cowboy/girl hats, boots, but tell them no play guns. (Keep extra bandanas in the classroom for students who have no special clothes to wear.)

- Make a campfire with sticks and crumpled orange bulletin board paper.

Sharing the Lesson

- Share the origin of the rodeo as contests on the ranch to see who had the best skill for each job to care for the livestock.

- Display the horseshoe and explain its purpose of protecting horses' feet. Tell the children that the ranch hands created games with things on the ranch. Pitching horseshoes is one example of reusing something instead of throwing it away when it's worn out. Model how to pitch the horseshoe, divide the group into teams, and play horseshoes.

- Explain the need to round up strays so the animals could be sold for money to buy new animals for the ranch. Demonstrate the Roping Strays activity, divide the group into teams, and compete.

- Discuss the cycle for penning livestock: come in for care and safety, back out to eat/graze. Demonstrate the Penning the Livestock event, divide the group into teams, and compete.

- Define the meaning of a chuck wagon: portable kitchen with food in a wagon. Demonstrate the Race to the Chuck Wagon event, divide the group into teams, and compete.

Checking for Understanding

- Direct rodeo contestants to circle round the campfire and enjoy a meal (snack packs) after a hard day's work at the rodeo.

- Explain that long ago cowboys/girls would gather around the campfire and share stories. Tell them that you will start the story, and then go around the circle so each child can add something to it.

Recommended Bibliography

Fiction

Cowboy Josè by Susan Middleton Elya. Putnam, 2005.

Cowboy Small by Lois Lenski. Random House, 2006.

Cowboy Up! by Larry Dane Brimner. Children's Press, 1999.

Cowgirl Kate and Cocoa by Erica Silverman. Harcourt, 2005.

Cowgirl Kate and Cocoa: Partners by Erica Silverman. Harcourt, 2006.

Cowgirl Kate and Cocoa: School Days by Erica Silverman. Harcourt, 2007.

Giddy up, Cowgirl by Jarrett Krosoczkra. Viking, 2006.

Lasso Lou and Cowboy McCoy by Barbara Larmon Failing. Dial, 2003.

Meanwhile Back at the Ranch by Trinka Hakes Noble. Puffin, 1992.

Nonfiction

Cowboy by Heather Miller. Heinemann Library, 2003.

I Wish I Were … a Cowboy by Ivan Bulloch. Two-Can, 1998.

Rodeo Time by Stuart J. Murphy. HarperCollins, 2006.

Web Sites

DLTK. www.dltk-teach.com. Go to the search box on the home page and type in "rodeo."

Everything Preschool. www.everythingpreschool.com/themes/western/index.htm. Western-themed preschool activities.

Pig Puppet Pattern

Copy the pattern onto cardstock/tagboard. Then color, cut out, and glue it to the top of a paint stick to create a stick puppet. For durability, laminate before gluing.

Chicken Puppet Pattern

Copy the pattern onto cardstock/tagboard. Then color, cut out, and glue it to the top of a paint stick to create a stick puppet. For durability, laminate before gluing.

Horse Puppet Pattern

Copy the pattern onto cardstock/tagboard. Then color, cut out, and glue it to the top of a paint stick to create a stick puppet. For durability, laminate before gluing.

Cow Puppet Pattern

Copy the pattern onto cardstock/tagboard. Then color, cut out, and glue it to the top of a paint stick to create a stick puppet. For durability, laminate before gluing.

I'M A LITTLE COWBOY/COWGIRL

(Sung to the tune of *I'm a Little Teapot*)

I'm a little  , watch me ride.

I herd the livestock back inside.

With my  and rope I can

wrestle a

just watch me rope and pull it near.

The Ranch Song

Sung to the tune of *Old MacDonald Had a Farm*.

Aileen Kirkham, ©2004

Cowboys and girls work on a ranch,

yipee ki yi yea, yee haw!

And on this ranch they care for livestock*,

yipee ki yi yea, yee haw!

With a roundup here and some roping there,

yipee ki yi yea, yee haw!

* For verses 2–5, change livestock to pigs,
chickens, horses and cows.

_____   _____   _____   _____

Sensational Senses: Opposites, Too

McRel Standards

Language Arts & Music

(Both listed in the Introduction on page 6.)

Science—Life Science

- Understands the structure and function of cells and organisms
- Understands the relationships among organisms and their physical environment

Thinking and Reasoning

- Understands and applies basic principles of logic and reasoning
- Effectively uses mental processes that are based on identifying similarities and differences

Working with Others

- Contributes to the overall effort of a group

Lesson Objectives

- Use scientific observation to define the purpose of the senses.
- Use the process of deduction to make a one-to-one correspondence between a body part and a sense.
- Identify the need for senses.
- Identify opposites.
- Experience the use of opposites in a variety of literary formats: poetry, books, games, etc.

Introduce the Lesson: Sensational Senses

Preparation

- Make a transparency of the song, *My Five Senses Will Never Lie* on page 142.

Presentation

- Direct the children to listen to the song carefully since they will need to decide which body part to point to when each verse is done: tongue, fingers, nose, eyes, and ears.
- Display the song, *My Five Senses Will Never Lie* on page 142.
- Demonstrate what they are to do by singing the first verse and then asking them what part should be pointed to.
- Sing each remaining verse, assess the students' understanding as they point to the parts, and discuss correct answers.

Check for Understanding

- Review the sense and body parts with students. You say the first part, then they finish the phrase and point/touch the body part.

  1. Taste with _____. (tongue/mouth)
  2. Touch with _____. (fingers/skin)
  3. Smell with _____. (nose)
  4. See with _____. (eyes)
  5. Hear with _____. (ears)

Sharing the Story Lesson

Preparation

- Select and display a variety of fiction and nonfiction about senses.
- Get a *Mr. Potato Head* toy.

Presentation

- Read aloud *My Five Senses* or *See, Hear, Smell, Taste, and Touch: Our Five Senses.*

- Explain that our senses are like a body's own telephone service that sends messages to our brain about what is happening to us.

Check for Understanding

- Tell the class they are going to play the *Mr. Potato Head Senses Game.*

- Divide the class into five groups.

- Tell them one person in their group gets to hold one part of Mr. Potato Head, but they all must vote with a yes or no shake of the head, for that person to add the part to Mr. Potato Head. If anyone in the group shakes their head "no," then the librarian/teacher must intervene to ask what other body part/sense that the no vote thinks it should be. Discuss.

- Give each group a sensory part to Mr. Potato Head: eyes, ears, nose, arms (fingers), and mouth (tongue).

- Ask the question, and then await the group's decision. The child with the piece should then come forward to place the part on Mr. Potato Head.

  Note: try to bring real objects (flower, bell, etc.) to make even more of a connection with this activity.

  1. What part smells a flower?
  2. What part hears a bell?
  3. What part sees a balloon?
  4. What part feels a kitty's fur?
  5. What part tastes a pickle?

- When all groups have added their pieces, ask who won the game to help Mr. Potato Head get his senses? (All of them did because they all helped Mr. Potato Head.) Congratulate the kids for being very SENSE-ABLE!

Extension Activity: Opposites, Too

Preparation

- Select and display a variety of fiction and nonfiction books about opposites including one of the following: *Mimi's Book of Opposites, Olivia's Opposites,* or *Swing High, Swing Low: A Day of Opposites.* All three of these titles show actions that young children have experienced in their personal worlds.

- Make transparency of the *Do You Know Your Opposites?* song.

Presentation

- Sing the action song *Do You Know Your Opposites?* on page 143.

- Read *Mimi's Book of Opposites, Olivia's Opposites,* or *Swing High, Swing Low: A Day of Opposites* aloud.

- As you read each set of opposite words, stop and repeat the first word of the opposite pair. Ask kids to identify the other opposite word that makes it a pair.

Check for Understanding

- Ask the students what they practiced today.

- Challenge students to fill in the blanks of opposites of pairs of words you generated that were not in the story. Say each example in a statement to let them fill in the word. Encourage them to demonstrate actions for each pair:

  1. If you're not fast like a rabbit, you must be _____ like a turtle. (slow)
  2. If you're not tall like a tree, you must be _____ like the grass. (short)
  3. If you're not big like a house, you must be _____ like a key. (little/small)
  4. If you're not loud like a horn, you must be _____ like a mouse. (quiet)
  5. If you're not hard like a rock, you must be _____ like a bunny. (soft)

Recommended Bibliography

Fiction

Can You See the Red Balloon? by Stella Blackstone. Barefoot Books, 2004.

Eric Carle's Opposites by Eric Carle. Penguin Putnam, 2007.

Goodnight, Sweet Pig by Linda Bailey. Kids Can Press, 2007. (Noise book, not taste.)

Hard Hat Area by Susan L. Roth. Bloomsbury Publishing, 2004.

If You See a Kitten by John Butler. Peachtree Publishers, 2002.

The Loud Family by Katherine Pebley O'Neal. Zonderkidz, 2008.

Maisy's Twinkly Crinkly Fun Book: Touch-and-Feel Fun! by Lucy Cousins. Candlewick Press, 2004.

Mimi's Book of Opposites by Emma Chichester Clark. Charlesbridge, 2003.

My Dog is as Smelly As Dirty Socks: And Other Family Portraits by Hanoch Piven. Schwartz & Wade Books, 2007.

Olivia's Opposites by Ian Falconer. Atheneum, 2002.

One Tractor: A Counting Book by Alexandra Siy. Holiday House, 2008.

Panda Bear, Panda Bear, What Do You See? by Bill Martin Jr. Henry Holt & Company, 2007.

Pat the Bunny by Dorothy Meserve Kunhardt. Golden Books, 2000.

Polar Bear, Polar Bear, What Do You Hear? by Bill Martin Jr. Holt, 1991.

Senses at the Seashore by Shelley Rotner. Millbrook Press, 2006.

Sweet Tooth by Margie Palatini. Simon & Schuster, 2004.

Swing High, Swing Low: A Book of Opposites by Fiona Coward. Barefoot Books, 2005.

Tasty Baby Belly Buttons by Judy Sierra. Random House, 2000.

Too Loud, Lily by Sophie Laguna. Scholastic, 2004.

There's a Nightmare in My Closet by Mercer Mayer. StoryTime Associates, 1991.

What Shall We Do with the Boo Hoo? Baby by Cressida Cowell. Mantra Lingua, 2002.

Nonfiction

Hot, Cold, Shy, Bold: Looking at Opposites by Pamela Harris. Kids Can Press, 1998.

Is the Treat Sour or Sweet? by Mary Elizabeth Salzmann. Abdo Pub., 2007.

Loud and Quiet: An Animal Opposites Book by Lisa Bullard. Capstone Press, 2007.

Loud Sounds, Soft Sounds by Patty Whitehouse. Rourke Publishing, 2007.

My Five Senses by Aliki. HarperCollins, 2000.

Our Senses by Susan Thames. Rourke Publishing, 2008.

Rocks: Hard, Soft, Smooth, and Rough by Natalie M. Rosinsky. Picture Window Books, 2003.

See, Hear, Smell, Taste, and Touch: Using Your Five Senses by Andrew Collins. National Geographic, 2006.

Smooth and Rough: An Animal Opposites Book by Lisa Bullard. Capstone Press, 2006.

Soft and Hard: An Animal Opposites Book by Nathan Olson. Capstone Press, 2008.

Super Senses by Shar Levine and Leslie Johnstone. Sterling Publishing, 2005.

The Sweet and Sour Animal Book by Langston Hughes. Oxford University Press, 1997.

Touch the Poem by Arnold Adoff. Blue Sky Press, 2000.

Use Your Senses by Melissa Stewart. Compass Point Books, 2005.

What Can I … Feel by Sue Barraclough. Raintree Steck-Vaughn, 2005.

What Can I … Hear by Sue Barraclough. Heinemann Library, 2005.

What Can I … See by Sue Barraclough. Heinemann Library, 2005.

What Can I … Smell by Sue Barraclough. Raintree Steck-Vaughn, 2005.

What Can I … Taste by Sue Barraclough. Raintree Steck-Vaughn, 2005.

Yum! A Book about Taste by Dana Meachen Rau. Picture Window Books, 2005.

Magazine

LibrarySparks "Fiction/Nonfiction: Sense-sational Selections," Vol. 5, No. 8, April 2008, p.53–55.

Web Sites

Jay Jay the Jet Plane: Caregiver's Corner. pbskids.org/jayjay/care.home.html. Lessons and activities.

Mr. Potato Head. www.hasbro.com/playskool/mrpotatohead. Purchase information and play tips.

Preschool Zone—Teaching Ideas. www.montgomeryschoolsmd.org/curriculum/pep/teach.htm. Click on "Opposites" to get an animated story of opposites.

TeachersAndFamilies Preschool Books. www.teachersandfamilies.com/open/psreading.cfm. Read the synopsis of the books listed on this site for more visual and auditory treats to read with preschool and kindergarten children.

My Five Senses Will Never Lie

Sung the tune of *How Much is That Doggie in the Window?*

Oh! What will I use to taste a pizza,
My tongue, or my nose, or my eyes?
Oh! What will I use to taste a pizza?
My five senses will never lie.

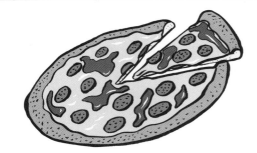

Oh! What do I use to touch a bunny,
My fingers, my tongue, or my eyes?
Oh! What do I use to touch a bunny?
My five senses will never lie.

Oh! What do I use to smell a diaper,
My fingers, my nose, or my eyes?
Oh! What do I use to smell a diaper?
My five senses will never lie.

Oh! What do I use to see an airplane,
My fingers, my tongue, or my eyes?
Oh! What do I use to see an airplane?
My five senses will never lie.

Oh! What do I use to hear some laughing,
My fingers, my ears, or my eyes?
Oh! What do I use to hear some laughing.
My five senses will never lie.

Do You Know Your Opposites?

Sing to the tune of *The Muffin Man;* demonstrate actions.

Aileen Kirkham, ©2009

Do you know your opposites,
your opposites, your opposites?
Do you know your opposites,
you see them every day.

To help you with your opposites,
your opposites, your opposites,
To help your with your opposites,
we'll practice them today.

Now it's time to open the book,
to open the book, to open the book,

Now it's time to open the book,
to read aloud today.

When we're done we'll shut the book,
we'll shut the book, we'll shut the book,

When we're done we'll shut the book,
that we read today.

Open and shut are opposites,
opposites, opposites.
Open and shut are opposites,
we'll practice them today.

Valuable Valentines: Mail Service Defined

McRel Standards

Language Arts & Music

(Both listed in the Introduction on page 6.)

Grades K-4 History: The History of Peoples of Many Cultures Around the World

- Understands the folklore and other cultural contributions from various regions of the United States and how they helped to form a national heritage

Life Work

- Studies or pursues specific job interests

Math

- Understands and applies basic and advanced properties of the concepts of numbers

Science—Life Science

- Understands relationships among organisms and their physical environment

Theatre

- Uses acting skills

Lesson Objectives

- Repeat the letter sound of V.
- Dramatize spatial vocabulary terms and animal movements.
- Identify animals specific to an African habitat.
- List specific locations within a hippopotamus' habitat.
- Repeat the rhythmic language in a rebus poem format.
- Participate in a repetitive pattern game.
- Reinforce colors and their names.

- Sequence the steps to send a valentine.
- Explore the role of postal workers.

Introduce the Lesson: Valuable Valentines

Preparation

- Make a transparency of the *V is for Valentine* song on page 147.

Presentation

- Display the words for *V is for Valentine*. Challenge them to tell you the letter sound of "v."
- Make note of the fact that when they see the verse, "v, v, v, v, v, v," they are to sing the letter sound instead of saying the letter name. Direct the children to echo sing the *V is for Valentine* song on page 147. Tell them you will sing first, and then they will repeat what you sing.

Sharing the Story Lesson

Preparation

- Select and display a variety of love-themed books for Valentine's Day lessons.
- Select two fiction books, one long and one short, from the bibliography. (My favorites are *I Love You: A Rebus Poem*. Kids can use the pictures to help read the words as a group. The other book I pair with this is *Kiss Kiss!* so kids can make the kissing sounds as a repetitive refrain after I read each page.)
- Cut out the five heart-shaped masks on pages 149–153. Glue them onto cardstock or poster board and color them with red and blue accents to accent the white paper. Laminate them to use year after year.
- Buy bags of small heart-shaped pretzels with the x in the middle, one per child in every class.

Presentation

- Seat the kids five to a row, sitting exactly one behind the other to play the pattern game in the "Check for Understanding" part of the lesson.

- Read aloud the valentine-themed stories about giving something that doesn't cost money: hugs, kisses, doing chores for loved ones, etc.

- Call on the the kids to name the ways we can show our family and friends we love them. Remind them to name gifts that DON'T cost money and list them as they are told.

- Share the fact that giving valentines to friends will take place in their classrooms.

Check for Understanding

- Use the transparency to sing the song again to reiterate the purpose of giving valentines on Valentine's Day.

- Ask the children what they will do in their classes to celebrate Valentine's Day.

- Tell the children that everyone at the library wants to show them how much they care about the kids, so the library will teach them a pattern game and give them a surprise.

- Show the kids the heart-shaped masks, and tell them that they will take turns passing them to their friends.

- Demonstrate by getting a child to come up and face you while you hold the mask in front of your face:

   (Hold mask in front of face, peek through eye holes and say line 1.)

   Valentines, valentines, red, white, and blue,

   (As you say line 2, pass the mask over the child and show how to place in front of face to see through eye holes.)

   I have a valentine to give to you.

- Play the game.

   1. Go to the first row of kids, tell them stand up and turn around to face the kids in the second row. Tell the second row kids to stand up and get ready to have the masks passed to them.

   2. Say the rhyme and assist row 1 passing to row 2.

   3. Help row 2 kids get the masks in place to peek through the eye holes and pass to row 3.

   4. Continue the pattern of saying the rhyme and passing to the back row. When you get to the last row, have the last row stay in line and follow you to stand in front of the first row so the last row of kids can have a turn passing the masks and the first row of kids has a turn to receive them.

   5. Pick up the masks.

- Challenge the kids to guess the tasty surprise they will receive by listening to the clue and seeing the drawing you make. Tell them they get three guesses and give extra clues as needed:

   1. Shaped like a heart. (Draw a heart on the board.)

   2. With lines criss-crossed. (Draw x inside of heart.)

   3. Instead of sugar, with salt we're glossed. (Add salt crystal shapes to heart shape and x.)

- Pass out the pretzels even if they guess incorrectly and wish them all a Happy Valentine's Day.

Extension Activity: How Valentines Are Mailed

Preparation

- Make a transparency of the *The Valentine Counting Song* found on page 148.

- Get the book, *Larabee*, and nonfiction books about the post office.

Sharing the Story Lesson

- Sing *The Valentine Counting Song.*

- Ask the students how they will "mail" their valentines to their school friends in their classes. (Usually each student has a container somewhere in the classroom to collect all their valentines.) Talk about the campus delivery method of dropping them in the container.

- Ask them how they would mail a valentine to someone who lived too far away to give it to them in person. Discuss responses.

- Read *Larabee* and/or picture-read a simplistic post office book aloud.

- Explain that each child sends and receives mail thanks to the postal worker, an essential community worker.

Checking for Understanding

- Sing *The Valentine Counting Song* again.

- Ask how valentines are delivered at school and to places far away where you can't go. Discuss responses to review correct answers.

- Restate the name of the place and the person who does faraway mail deliveries: post office, postal worker, or mail carrier.

  Optional: liaison with the upper grade teachers to make arrangements for their older students to go to the Pre-K and Kinder classes during the valentines exchange so the older students can read the valentines to the little ones.

Recommended Bibliography

Fiction

1,2,3 Valentine's Day by Jeanne Modesitt. Boyds Mills Press, 2004.

Be Mine, Be Mine, Sweet Valentine by Sarah Weeks. Laura Geringer Books, 2006.

The Bear Hug by Sean Callahan. Albert Whitman, 2006.

Do You Want a Hug, Honey Bunny? by Rachael O'Neill. Tiger Tales, 2008.

How About a Hug? by Nancy Carlson. Viking, 2001.

How Do I Love You? by Leslie Kimmelman. HarperCollins, 2006.

I Will Kiss You (Lots & Lots & Lots!) by Stuart E. Hample. Candlewick Press, 2006.

If You'll Be My Valentine by Cynthia Rylant. HarperCollins, 2005.

Kiss Kiss! by Margaret Wild. Simon & Schuster, 2004.

Rhyme Time Valentine by Nancy Poydar. Holiday House, 2003.

Larabee by Kevin Luthardt. Peachtree Publishers, 2004.

Sweet Hearts by Jan Carr. Holiday House, 2003.

Valentines Are for Saying I Love You by Margaret Sutherland. Grosset & Dunlap, 2007.

Where's My Hug? by James Mayhew. Bloomsbury Publishing, 2008.

Nonfiction

Delivering Your Mail: A Book about Mail Carriers by Ann Owen. Picture Window Books, 2004.

I Love You! A Bushel & a Peck: Taken from the Song "A Bushel and a Peck" by Frank Loesser. HarperCollins, 2005.

I Love You: A Rebus Poem by Jean Marzollo. Scholastic, 2000.

I Love You: Verses & Sweet Sayings by Bessie Pease Gutmann. Grosset & Dunlap, 2007.

Out and About at the Post Office by Kitty Shea. Picture Window Books, 2004.

Valentine's Day Is … by Gail Gibbons. Holiday House, 2006.

Web Site

- Billy Bear's Happy Valentine's Day for Kids, Family and Teachers. www.billybear4kids.com/holidays/valentin/fun.htm. Click on Online Games, then Ziffle the Valentine's Pony "Easy Drop and Drag." This provides the opportunity to solve from parts to whole, which addresses spatial concepts with young children.

V is for Valentine

Sung to the tune of *Frère Jacques.*

Aileen Kirkham, ©1999

V is for valentine.

V is for valentine.

V, v, v,

V, v, v,

Valentines are very nice.

Valentines are very nice

To share with all of you,

To share with all of you.

The Valentine Counting Song

Sing to the tune of *10 Little Indians,* and demonstrate actions.

Aileen Kirkham, ©2009

(Count by holding up fingers.)

1 little, 2 little, 3 little valentines,
4 little, 5 little, 6 little valentines,
7 little, 8 little, 9 little valentines,
They need to be mailed by you.

(Use a real envelope to demonstrate stuffing a valentine.)

Don't forget to stuff them with good wishes,
Don't forget to stuff them with good wishes,
Don't forget to stuff them with good wishes,
They need to be mailed by you.

(Pretend to kiss, kiss, kiss the back of the envelope.)

Don't forget to seal them all with kisses,
Don't' forget to seal them all with kisses,
Don't forget to seal them all with kisses,
They need to be mailed by you.

Heart-Shaped Mask Pattern

Cut out the five heart-shaped masks on the following pages. Glue them onto cardstock or poster board and color them with red and blue accents to accent the white paper.
Laminate them to use year after year.

Heart-Shaped Mask Pattern

Heart-Shaped Mask Pattern

Heart-Shaped Mask Pattern

Heart-Shaped Mask Pattern

When I Grow Up: Community Helpers

McRel Standards

Language Arts & Music

(Both listed in the Introduction on page 6.)

Behavioral Studies

- Understands conflict, cooperation, and interdependence among individuals, groups, and institutions

Civics—What are the Roles of the Citizen in American Democracy

- Understands how participation in civic and political life can help citizens attain individual and public goals

Health

- Knows the availability and effective use of health services, products, and Information

Life Work

- Studies or pursues specific job interests

Theatre

- Uses acting skills

Working With Others

- Contributes to the overall effort of a group
- Works well with diverse individuals in diverse situations

Lesson Objectives

- Define the role of community helpers.
- Identify the cause and effect economics of work for pay.

- Describe the role of various community helpers.
- Participate in a program to develop public speaking skills.

Introduce the Lesson: When I Grow Up

Preparation

- Optional—make the firefighter puppet on page 158 to sing the song to introduce the lesson.
- Make a transparency of the *When I Grow Up!* song on page 159 for students to see and sing along.
- Copy the Family Program Note found on page 160.
- Bookmark the Play Safe, Be Safe! Web site: www.playsafebesafe.com.

Presentation

- Display the song transparency and ask the students if they know who these community helpers are. Give clues as needed to fill in the blanks under each person.
- Direct the children to echo sing the song *When I Grow Up* on page 159. Tell them you will sing first, then they will repeat what you sang.

Sharing the Story Lesson

Preparation

- Select and display a variety of community helper books.
- Select a fiction book from the bibliography.

Presentation

- Read the book aloud with emphasis on the role of the firefighter. (Two of the best: *Even Firefighters Hug Moms* and *Fireman Small: Fire Down Below!*)

- Picture read a nonfiction book about firefighters and their jobs

  OR

- Open the bookmarked Web site and do the activities as a group to learn about fire fighters and fire safety.

- It has been documented that young children have been frightened by firefighters in uniform and have hidden from them, resulting in the childrens' deaths. Making children aware of what to expect in an emergency can help prevent tragedy. **Emphasize that firefighters dress in special suits with gear and masks**. Children need to know that a firefighter can look scary, but firefighters are trained to wear the special suits and masks because that is the safest way for them to walk through the fire to find people.

Check for Understanding

- Use the transparency to sing the song again to reiterate the role of community helpers.

- Challenge students to name other community helpers, and give clues as needed:

  1. This community helper cares for your teeth.

  2. This community helper picks up your garbage.

  3. This community helper delivers your mail.

  4. This community helper tells or shows you where to find good books.

  5. This community helper enforces the law and directs traffic.

  6. This community helper takes care of sick and injured animals.

- Encourage students to check out community helper books to picture read and read alouds with their families and friends.

Extension Activity: When I Grow Up

- Direct the children to each name a job a parent/family member has and identify how it helps the community.

- Record their answers and then ask them to pick which job they would like to have when they grow up.

- Ask students if their parents get paid for their job and why parents need to be paid. Discuss as necessary for students to understand economics of employment.

- Tell students they will have the opportunity to dress up as their favorite (or their parent's) occupation.

- Show them the take-home letter on page 160 and explain that it will tell their parents to dress them in the clothing of their favorite/parent's occupations for a school program.

- Pass out letters and watch students put them in their backpacks so they don't get left at school.

Prior to the program, have the students practice a simple statement for each one of them to say at the program. Tell them you will announce their names one by one to come forward to say their part for the program and reassure them that you will help them as needed:

When I grow up, I want to be a

_____

to help people _____

_____ .

Recommended Bibliography

Fiction

Apple Farmer Annie by Monica Wellington. Puffin, 2004.

The Boy Who Was Raised By Librarians by Carla Morris. Peachtree Publishers, 2007.

Clifford to the Rescue by Norman Bridwell. Scholastic, 2000.

Digger Man by Andrea Griffing Zimmerman. Henry Holt & Company, 2007.

D.W.'s Library Card by Marc Tolon Brown. Little, Brown and Company, 2001.

Even Firefighters Hug Their Moms by Christine Kole MacLean. Puffin, 2004.

Fireman Small: Fire Down Below! by Wong Herbert Yee. Houghton Mifflin, 2001.

Froggy Goes to the Doctor by Jonathan London. Viking, 2002.

Good Morning, Digger by Anne Rockwell. Viking, 2005.

Grandma Drove the Garbage Truck by Katie Clark. Down East Books, 2005.

Harry and the Dinosaurs Say "Raahh!" by Ian Whybrow. Random House, 2004.

I.Q. Goes to the Library by Mary Ann Fraser. Walker & Co., 2003.

I Hate to be Sick! by Aamir Lee Bermiss. Scholastic, 2004.

I'm Dirty by Kate McMullan. Joanna Cotler Books, 2006.

I Stink! by Kate McMullan. Weston Woods, 2004.

Larabee by Kevin Luthardt. Peachtree Publishers, 2004.

Little Rabbit's Loose Tooth by Lucy Bate. Knopf, 2006.

Mother, Mother, I Feel Sick, Send for the Doctor, Quick, Quick, Quick by Remy Charlip and Burton Supree. Tricycle Press, 2001.

A Small Christmas by Wong Herbert Lee. Houghton Mifflin, 2007.

Smash! Mash! Crash! There Goes the Trash! by Barbara Odanaka. Margaret K. McElderry Books, 2006.

Nonfiction

ABC Letters in the Library by Bonnie Farmer. Lobster Press, 2005.

The Farmer in the Dell published by David R. Godine, 2004.

Field Trips series published by Picture Window Books:

- *Out and About at the Bakery* by Jennifer A. Ericsson. 2003.
- *Out and About at the Bank* by Nancy Garham Attebury. 2006.
- *Out and About at the Dairy Farm* by Andy Murphy. 2003.
- *Out and About at the Dentist* by Bitsy Kemper. 2007.
- *Out and About at the Fire Station* by Muriel L. Dubois. 2003.
- *Out and About at the Hospital* by Nancy Garhan Attebury. 2006.
- *Out and About at the Post Office* by Kitty Shea. 2004.
- *Out and About at the Public Library* by Kitty Shea. 2006.
- *Out and About at the Supermarket* by Kitty Shea. 2004.
- *Out and About at the Vet Clinic* by Kitty Shea. 2004.
- *Out and About at the Zoo* by Kathleen W. Deady. 2003.

First Facts: Community Helpers at Work series, Capstone Press:

- *A Day in the Life of a Child Care Worker* by Heather Adamson. 2004.

- *A Day in the Life of a Construction Worker* by Heather Adamson. 2004.

- *A Day in the Life of a Dentist* by Heather Adamson. 2004.

- *A Day in the Life of a Doctor* by Heather Adamson. 2004.

- *A Day in the Life of a Farmer* by Heather Adamson. 2004.

- *A Day in the Life of a Firefighter* by Heather Adamson. 2004.

- *A Day in the Life of a Garbage Collector* by Nate LeBoutillier. 2005.

- *A Day in the Life of a Librarian* by Judy Monroe. 2005.

- *A Day in the Life of a Nurse* by Connie Fluet. 2005.

- *A Day in the Life of a Police Officer* by Heather Adamson. 2004.

- *A Day in the Life of a Teacher* by Heather Adamson. 2004.

- *A Day in the Life of a Veterinarian* by Heather Adamson. 2004.

- *A Day in the Life of a Zookeeper* by Nate LeBoutillier. 2005.

- *A Day in the Life of an Emergency Medical Technician* by Heather Adamson. 2004.

Hush, Little Digger by Ellen Olson-Brown. Tricycle Press, 2006.

Professional Books

Goldie Socks and the Three Libearians by Jackie Mims Hopkins. UpstartBooks, 2007.

Web Site

- Play Safe! Be Safe! www.playsafebesafe.com. Fire safety games and activities for grades PK–1. Offers language options in English, French, and Spanish.

Firefighter Puppet Pattern

Copy the pattern onto cardstock/tagboard. Then color, cut out, and glue it to the top of a paint stick to create a stick puppet. For durability, laminate before gluing.